"Perennial dieters! Compulsive calorie counters! Weight Watchers dropouts! You are *my* kind of people and this is *our* literary event of the decade: *The Brand-Name Calorie Counter.* A beacon lights three centuries of nutritional murk. With the dedication of a scientist, Corinne Netzer has penetrated the caloric mystery of the supermarket."

Gael Greene, Life Magazine

". . . help has appeared in a paperback book that takes note of supermarket realities. It's *The Brand-Name Calorie Counter.* Now those who are overweight can count calories in almost all prepared or convenience foods—and compare various brands as well."

Morris Fishbein, M.D., Medical World News

Expanded!

THE BRAND-NAME CALORIE COUNTER

by CORINNE T. NETZER
with ELAINE CHABACK

A DELL BOOK

Published by
Dell Publishing Co., Inc.
1 Dag Hammarskjold Plaza
New York, New York 10017

Dell ® TM 681510, Dell Publishing Co., Inc.
Printed in the United States of America

Previous Dell Edition—#0776

ISBN: 0-440-10776-8

New Dell Edition
First printing—June 1971
Second printing—September 1971
Third printing—May 1972
Fourth printing—September 1972
Fifth printing—February 1973
Sixth printing—April 1973
Seventh printing—January 1974
Eighth printing—April 1974
Ninth printing—May 1975
Tenth printing—July 1975
Eleventh printing—January 1976
Twelfth printing—June 1976
Thirteenth printing—August 1976
Fourteenth printing—November 1976
Fifteenth printing—January 1977

ACKNOWLEDGMENTS

A book of this scope can't be the work of only one person, or even one hundred persons. To explore a field as large as the food industry means relying almost entirely on the goodwill and cooperation of the industry itself. Without that assistance, *The Brand-Name Calorie Counter* couldn't have been compiled; therefore, I wish to acknowledge my deep indebtedness to every company that contributed to this book.

In addition, I'm indebted to specific people within many companies who responded to what must have seemed endless requests for further data and clarification. Among the home economists, laboratory, public relations and other personnel to whom I'm specially grateful are Dorothy Holland (Kraftco), Ellanora Valle (General Foods), Paul Kahn (ITT Continental Baking Co.,), Claire Boasi (Campbell Soup Co.), Walter Kough (American Home Foods), William Bokman (Kitchens of Sara Lee), Ed Bernardoni (Beatrice Foods Co.), Eleanor Bazata (Sealtest Foods), Doloris Cogan (Pepperidge Farms), Joseph McDonnell, Jr. (Borden Inc.), Dr. Stuart Itter (Standard Brands Inc.), Shirley O'Neil (Hunt-Wesson Foods), Dr. F. C. Hildebrand (General Mills, Inc.), Phyllis Lovrien (Oscar Mayer & Co.), Mary Ellen Jenks (Green Giant Co.), Jean Carol (R. J. Reynolds Inc.), Ruth Burke (R. T. French Co.), Everett Maguire (Thomas J. Lipton, Inc.), and Madeleine Hall (Durkee Famous Foods).

I am also grateful to Meg Raben for her monumental efforts in helping to organize and clarify the material.

PREFACE

My concern with overweight is personal as well as professional. Speaking as a man who suffered a heart attack twenty years ago, I know I wouldn't be alive today if, following that attack, I hadn't taken off fifty excess pounds in a hurry. Speaking as a practicing physician, I am convinced that overweight is this nation's Number One health problem. Bear in mind that among the serious disorders affected adversely by overweight are coronary heart disease, peripheral vascular disease, high blood pressure, diabetes, and hardening of the arteries. Very simply, overweight is a kind of death for almost everyone—slow for some, quicker for others.

In my fifty years of medical practice, I have treated over 10,000 overweight men and women. Readers who are familiar with my book *The Doctor's Quick Weight Loss Diet* are aware that I believe in fast-action dieting—particularly for people who have failed to reduce (or to stay reduced) on slow-action plans. The Quick Weight Loss Diet has been the most effective method used by my patients; however, I have seen dozens of other fast-action diets work with equal success. As I have stated time and time again, what matters most is to *get that fat off fast*—on whatever diet suits you best. Naturally, anyone with a serious physical disorder should reduce only under the close supervision of a doctor; however, the main problem of the majority of those who are too heavy is "simple overactive fork!" This majority *can* go on a quick-reducing diet for limited periods without fear of impairing their health; this majority should know that what *is* impairing their health is all those extra pounds!

I've consented to write a preface to *The Brand-Name Calorie Counter* because I'm overjoyed at the contents of this book. Indeed, it is my belief that in answering questions that doctors and dieters alike have asked for years, *The Brand-Name Calorie Counter* may revolutionize the whole process of reducing! In the past, those of us concerned about weight have been largely in the dark about the caloric content of hundreds of foods that line the shelves of every supermarket. Because we lacked information—and because calories *do* count—we were forced to exclude many of these foods from our patients' diets. Thanks to *The Brand-Name Calorie*

Counter, we are no longer in the dark. Finally, doctor and dieter can determine, *accurately,* how to broaden the scope of any diet. Every bit as important, the calorie listings in this book will help those who have already reduced to stay reduced!

There can be little doubt that ignorance about what we eat has contributed greatly to the national problem of overweight. *The Brand-Name Calorie Counter* offers all of us much needed enlightenment. Professionals in the field of health, as well as the general public, will benefit greatly from the information herein.

IRWIN M. STILLMAN, M.D.

INTRODUCTION

I had two reasons for starting this book: twenty excess pounds and a ton of sheer frustration. I'd gained those extra pounds in less than a year, and, for the first time in my life, I was faced with the problems of dieting and counting calories.

As a new dieter, I had a lot to learn, all of it the hard way. Despite the promises of numerous magazines and books, I didn't find reducing "actually pleasant," nor did I benefit one iota from dozens of "diet tips and tricks." Cutting three ounces of lean broiled meat into paper-thin slices didn't fool *my* stomach into believing the portion was bigger. Sprinkling vegetables with oregano, tarragon, cumin, basil, dill weed, and thyme added a dash of flavor, but the food wasn't a bit more filling. Garnishing a chicken wing with watercress created a "festive" atmosphere, but I still left the table dissatisfied.

At the end of my first week of dieting, I think the main thing I'd learned is that the average diet is made up of many adjectives and little food. For example, when you're reducing, lettuce is never simply lettuce. It is "a wedge of crispy, garden-fresh lettuce"—or when topped with a goody such as skim-milk cottage cheese, it is "a bed of crispy, garden-fresh. . . ." ("Tangy" is the most popular adjective of diet writers, but it is followed close on the heels by "crispy," "zesty," "tempting," and "savory.")

At the end of two weeks, I was slimmer by six pounds, but my disposition was a disaster. It was bad enough restricting how much I ate, but I resented even more giving up many favorite foods because I didn't know their caloric content. Very simply, I wanted more choice in what I ate. Instead of half a medium cantaloupe for dessert, could I satisfy my sweet tooth with a Baby Ruth nugget? In place of four ounces of broiled halibut steak ("garnished with fresh parsley"), could I substitute a slice of Chef Boy-Ar-Dee frozen pizza?

None of the calorie counters I'd bought had answers to these questions. They simply didn't acknowledge the existence of hundreds—indeed, thousands—of packaged foods. Most calorie counters listed pretzels, peanuts, and potato chips, but where could I find Whistles, Bugles, Buttons and Bows? And what about Popsicles, Pop Tarts, Tang, Mott's A.M. and P.M.? What about Chinese foods, packaged dip mixes, flavored rice, TV dinners—perhaps 50 percent of the foods on the shelves of every supermarket?

My doctor had told me that it was all right to make up my own 1000-calories-a-day diet, but how could I? I didn't have the information I needed to decide how to "spend" my precious calories.

And so the compilation of this book began—and, like Topsy, it grew and grew. Originally, I'd set out simply to learn the caloric content of foods ignored by ordinary calorie counters, but as the data poured in, it became clear that the job was far bigger—and more fascinating—than I'd imagined.

For instance, consider a common processed food such as corned beef hash. Six national brands are listed in this book—each with a different caloric content! Why are they all different? For the same reason that the tuna fish salad you make at home probably contains greater or fewer calories than the tuna fish salad made by your neighbor: You use different recipes! Perhaps your family likes tuna salad with diced pickle while your neighbor's family prefers it with celery. Perhaps your family likes a lot of mayonnaise in tuna salad while your neighbor's family likes only a little. For these reasons, or a dozen others, the chances are slim that your tuna fish salad contains exactly the same number of calories as your neighbor's.

The same reasoning applies to the majority of foods we buy in a store. Each producer follows a different recipe; therefore, though many companies may make the "same" food, individual brands are likely to differ in caloric content and taste. This difference in recipes, by the way, explains why each of us has a favorite brand of so many foods.

Despite what anyone says, I don't believe dieting is ever painless (let alone "actually pleasant"), but I do believe the information herein can make the whole dreary business a good deal easier. In particular, this information can help relieve the dismal sameness of most reducing menus. For example, if you're allowed 400-500 calories for dinner, you'll find there are dozens of alternatives to those old diet standbys: broiled fish, liver, chicken, and beef. Swanson's frozen ham TV dinner has 366 calories; Chun King's frozen egg foo young has 240 calories per package, and their frozen chicken chow mein dinner, 352 calories. I've never seen a diet that includes spaghetti, yet a full cup of Spaghetti-O's (with tomato-cheese sauce!) has only 200 calories. An 8-ounce package of Banquet's frozen macaroni and cheese has 280 calories; a cup of Kraft's Noodles Romanoff (noodles with beef, sour cream and cheese sauce) has 478 calories!

Just for the record, let me state clearly that I'm not an expert on reducing or nutrition, and the aim of this book isn't to suggest to readers how to lose weight. The kind of diet you undertake is a matter for you to decide by yourself—or, if there's any question about your health, with the help of a physician. The sole purpose of *The Brand-Name Calorie Counter* is to take some of the mystery (and misery) out of diet eating.

I hope you'll find most of your favorite brands included herein; however, the limitations of time and space are bound to cause some disappointments. In general, I've tried to list those products which are best known and most widely distributed; more specifically, few, if any, well-known brands are missing, though not every food of every company may be included. For example, the book contains data on Morton's frozen corn and blueberry muffins, but it doesn't list the company's English muffins. Why? Simply because the Morton lab wasn't able to complete an analysis of the product in time for this edition. Speaking of laboratory analysis of food, it's expensive—very expensive. Many smaller companies couldn't provide data on their products because they had no home economics department, and the cost of outside analysis was prohibitive.

If you're truly unhappy that some of your favorite foods aren't listed, I suggest writing directly to the producers. For fast results, address your request to the president of the company. He may not have the information you want, but he'll forward it to the right department (and a letter forwarded by the president usually gets a faster reply than mail that comes in "cold").

The Brand-Name Calorie Counter will help anyone who is weight conscious—people who are simply trying not to gain as well as people who are trying to reduce. In truth, I find that I use the material even more now than I did while I was dieting. I watch what I eat, but I eat what I want. I haven't regained the pounds I lost because I know, almost exactly, how many calories I'm consuming.

As you will see, there are many ways in which to utilize the information in this book. For example, you may decide to make substitutions on whatever diet you're following (anyone for 34 Jujubes in place of "2 crispy stalks celery and a cup chilled sauerkraut juice"?); you may decide to try new foods and/or new brands; you may decide *not* to change your diet by as much as a garden-fresh carrot strip. But whatever you decide, the choice will be yours, based on a new—and accurate—knowledge of calories. This is the book that takes the guesswork out of dieting; it may also be the book that leads to your attaining, *and* maintaining, your proper weight.

C. T. N.

P.S. In order to include as many "regular" foods as possible, I haven't listed any diet foods (No-Cal, for example) in *The Brand-Name Calorie Counter.* I've never seen a diet food that didn't have a label stating the product's caloric content; therefore, it seemed to me that I'd be cheating readers if I included this group of foods in the book.

CONTENTS

continued

HOW TO USE THIS BOOK

I suppose there are people who can actually determine what constitutes "one average serving beef stew" or "two thin slices roast lamb" or "one small wedge watermelon." But measures of this kind utterly bewilder me—and, more important, they are unacceptable to home economists, nutritionists, and others in the food industry. The whole point of any diet is to know what you're eating; therefore, the measures used throughout this book are as exact as possible.

Fortunately, the majority of foods are listed in an everyday household measure, or in a size as packaged by the producer. However, in the latter case, I can't emphasize enough the importance of being aware that similar foods aren't necessarily packaged in the same size. For example, consider Nabisco's two brands of chocolate-covered marshmallow cookies, Pinwheels and Mallomars. I've listed all cookies by the piece (one cookie, as packaged), and if you check, you'll find that a Pinwheel has 139 calories, a Mallomar, 60 calories. However, while it is true that one Pinwheel has more than twice as many calories as one Mallomar, it is also true that a pound of Pinwheels contains 2 calories less than a pound of Mallomars! The answer to this seeming mystery is simple: The size of one Pinwheel is more than double the size of one Mallomar. By the ounce or by the pound, the caloric content of the two brands is nearly identical.

To get the most from *The Brand-Name Calorie Counter,* you must recognize that you can't always use the book to compare foods that are similar. Specifically, when products are listed in a size "as packaged," you can't compare brands unless you are certain that the sizes are the same. *If you're not certain, don't make comparisons; they may not be accurate.*

You can, of course, compare any foods that are listed in the *same* standard measure. This means you can compare the calories in a half cup spinach with the calories in a half cup lima beans; or the calories in one ounce chocolate with the calories in one ounce lemon drops. However, what you *can't* do (and it took me forever to understand this) is compare foods that are listed in a dissimilar unit of measure. For example, don't compare four ounces chili con carne with half a cup boiled rice. Why? Because "four ounces" is a measure of *weight* and "half a cup" is a meaure of *capacity* (how much space the food—or anything else—occupies).

Try to think about it this way: Eight ounces of puffed rice is *not* the same as an eight-ounce cup of puffed rice. Eight ounces of the cereal contains 785 calories—and would fill almost 19 standard measuring cups! An eight-ounce cup of puffed rice has 45 calories—and holds less than half an ounce of the cereal! See what I mean about not comparing dissimilar units of measure?

An overwhelming number of people, including some doctors, mistakenly believe that a cup holds eight ounces, a half cup holds four ounces, etc. As I hope I've shown, that simply isn't true. It *can* be true (for example, eight ounces of butter fills the capacity of an eight-ounce cup); however, it's just as likely to be false.

What an eight-ounce cup does hold is eight *fluid* ounces. But fluid ounces aren't a measure of weight; they are a measure of capacity *only*. (If you really want to get technical, the capacity of eight fluid ounces is 14.4 cubic inches!) Therefore, final warning, you can't accurately compare a food listed by weight with a food listed by capacity.

As noted before, you can, of course, compare foods listed in a similar measure—and you can, of course, convert a unit of measure to a smaller or larger amount. You may find the charts below helpful in making conversions.

EQUIVALENTS BY CAPACITY
(all measurements level)

1 quart	=	4 cups
1 cup	=	8 fluid ounces
	=	½ pint
	=	16 tablespoons
2 tablespoons	=	1 fluid ounce
1 tablespoon	=	3 teaspoons

EQUIVALENTS BY WEIGHT

1 pound	=	16 ounces
3.57 ounces	=	100 grams
1 ounce	=	28.35 grams

You don't have to know that there are 28.35 grams in an ounce to use this book, but you may find the information handy when shopping or comparing package sizes. By federal law, the net weight (or volume) of a packaged food must be printed on the food's can, box, wrapping, etc. Most containers list a food's net weight in ounces or pounds; however, you'll occasionally come across a label that reads—for example—"Net Weight 222 grams." The only way you can determine that the net weight of that food is somewhat less than eight ounces is by knowing how many grams equal one ounce.

By the way, if you haven't paid attention to package sizes before, now is a good time to start. Indeed, if you don't start, you won't get full value out of some important sections of *The Brand-Name Calorie Counter*. For example, the book lists the caloric content of all varieties of candy by the ounce—which means that to find out how many calories are in a chocolate bar, package of caramels, etc., you must determine the candy's net weight. Hershey's milk chocolate, for instance, contains 152 calories per ounce, and is available in four different size bars. Check the wrapper on any size to learn the net weight of the candy; multiply the number of ounces by 152, and you'll know the caloric content of the bar. (Presently, the net weight of the popular 10¢-size Hershey is 1¼ ounces; thus it contains 190 calories. However, because of fluctuations in the price of cocoa, the sizes of all brands of chocolate bars often change; therefore, the net weight should always be checked.)

You'll find many products in *The Brand-Name Calorie Counter* that require some home preparations—cake mixes, condensed soups, etc. For convenience—and, more important, for accuracy—most of these foods are listed prepared, *according to package directions.* I stress "according to package directions" because if you vary the directions, you may change the caloric content of the food. For example, you'll find that a cup of Campbell's cream of mushroom soup contains 217 calories "prepared according to package directions, *with whole fresh milk.*" However, if you make this soup (or any other condensed cream soup) with skim milk, it will have 25 to 40 fewer calories per cup; and should you use water in place of milk, the soup will have about 80 less calories per cup!

I don't, of course, mean to imply that you must follow package directions (especially if a change results in cutting down on calories); I just hope you'll remember that variations in preparation can affect the caloric content of foods listed "prepared according to package directions."

To get the most from your diet, bear in mind that all measures in this book are level: 1 *level* teaspoon, 1 *level* cup, etc. Your diet won't be ruined if your own measures aren't always level, but if you cheat consistently, you surely won't lose as fast.

As I've said before, I don't think this book—or any book—can make dieting easy. But I do think *The Brand-Name Calorie Counter* makes dieting less depressing, eating more interesting! I can't swear I wouldn't have reduced without the information herein; I *can* swear I reduced faster—and have been able to maintain my weight—because of this information. I sincerely believe the book can do the same for you.

Finally, these last words about calories and brand-name foods. Home economists in the food industry (like good cooks anywhere) may improve the way in which a food is processed or produced—and, as a result, the caloric content may change. In addition, economic factors sometimes cause a difference in how a food is packaged (for example, the size of a cookie may decrease or increase) and, therefore, the caloric content may change. As *The Brand-Name Calorie Counter* goes to press, all figures are up to date, but it's impossible to guarantee that some won't change. When necessary, corrections will be made in later editions of the book; however, if one of your favorite foods is suddenly labeled "New; Improved," or if there is a difference in its size, you may want to write to the producer to ask if the caloric content is still the same.

ABBREVIATIONS USED IN THIS BOOK

fl.	fluid	swt.	sweetened
lb.	pound	tbsp.	tablespoon
oz.	ounce	tsp.	teaspoon
"	inch	w/	with
pkg.	package	wo/	without

BREADSTUFFS, CRACKERS AND FLOUR PRODUCTS 1

BREAD, 1 slice, as packaged, except as noted

See also "Rolls and Muffins" and page 121

Be careful about comparing the calories in brands of pre-sliced bread. Remember, bread is packaged in different size slices and, to be accurate, you must be sure you're comparing slices of the same size. (See "How to Use This Book," pages xv-xviii.)

	CALORIES
brown, w/raisins, canned (B & M), ½" slice	90
corn, mix, prepared* (Aunt Jemima), 2¾" x 2⅝" x 1¼" slice	224
corn and molasses (Pepperidge Farm)	71
cracked wheat (Pepperidge Farm)	66
cracked wheat (Tasty-Bake)	70
date nut (Thomas')	100
French, brown and serve, baked (Pepperidge Farm), ¾" slice	79
gluten (Thomas' Glutogen)	35
Italian, brown and serve, baked (Pepperidge Farm), ¾" slice	81
oatmeal (Pepperidge Farm)	66
(Profile)	52
protein (Thomas' Protogen)	45
pumpernickel (Pepperidge Farm)	79
raisin (Thomas' English)	66
raisin, cinnamon (Pepperidge Farm)	76
raisin, cinnamon (Thomas')	63
rye (Pepperidge Farm)	82
rye (Tasty-Bake)	91
wheat germ (Pepperidge Farm Hovis Golden Sandwich)	68
white:	
(Daffodil Farm)	58
(Pepperidge Farm—large)	77
(Pepperidge Farm—sandwich)	71
(Pepperidge Farm English Tea Loaf)	71
(Tasty-Bake)	72

white bread, continued

(Thomas') 64
(Wonder) 64
whole wheat (Pepperidge Farm) 61
whole wheat (Thomas') 65

* *According to package directions*

BREADSTICKS, 1 piece, as packaged

	CALORIES
plain (Stella D'Oro)	40
onion flavored (Stella D'Oro)	36
sesame (Stella D'Oro)	38

ROLLS & MUFFINS, 1 piece, as packaged, except as noted

See also "Miscellaneous Baked Products" and page 121

To compare the calories in different brands and types of rolls and muffins, you should be certain you're comparing products that are the same size. Otherwise, your comparisons are likely to be inaccurate. (See "How to Use This Book," pages xv-xviii.)

	CALORIES
biscuits, refrigerator, baked (Borden's Big 10 Flaky)	83
biscuits, buttermilk, refrigerator, baked (Borden's)	57
biscuits, sweetmilk, refrigerator, baked (Borden's Southern Style)	57
muffins:	
blueberry, frozen (Howard Johnson's Toastees)	118
bran (Thomas' Toast-r-Cakes)	118
corn (Thomas')	180
corn (Thomas' Toast-r-Cakes)	114
corn, frozen (Howard Johnson's Toastees)	118
corn, mix, prepared* (Flako), 2½" diameter	135
English (Cain's)	145
English (Di Carlo)	145
English (Hostess)	145
English (Thomas')	140
English (Wonder)	145
orange, frozen (Howard Johnson's Toastees)	115
popovers, mix, prepared* (Flako), 1 popover, 3" diameter	166
rolls:	
hard, brown and serve, baked (Pepperidge Farm Club)	120
hard, brown and serve, baked (Pepperidge Farm French), 3-oz. size	264

hard, brown and serve, baked (Pepperidge Farm French) 5-oz. size ... 389
hard, brown and serve, baked (Pepperidge Farm Hearth) ... 64
hard, brown and serve, baked (Wonder) ... 80
hard, w/sesame seeds, brown and serve, baked
(Pepperidge Farm Sesame Crisp) ... 75
soft (Pepperidge Farm Dinner) ... 80
soft, brown and serve, baked (Pepperidge Farm Golden Twist) ... 123
soft, refrigerator, baked (Borden's Gem Flake) ... 70
soft, onion-flavored, refrigerator, baked
(Borden's Onion Crescent Flaky) ... 95
scones (Hostess) ... 188

* *According to package directions*

CRACKERS, 1 piece, as packaged, except as noted

See also "Cracker Sandwiches" and page 122

Bear in mind that crackers are available in dozens of sizes and shapes; therefore, it is hard—indeed, often impossible—to accurately compare the caloric content of different brands and types. (See "How to Use This Book," pages xv-xviii.)

CALORIES

bacon flavored (Nabisco Bacon Thins) ... 11
barbecue flavored (Chit Chat) ... 14
barbecue flavored (Sunshine Barbecue Snack Wafers) ... 17
butter flavored:
(Keebler Butter Thins) ... 17
(Hi-Ho) ... 17
(Keebler Club) ... 15
(Keebler Townhouse) ... 19
(Nabisco Butter Thins) ... 15
(Ritz) ... 18
(Tam-Tams) ... 13
butter-cheese flavored (Ritz Cheese) ... 18
caraway (Caraway Crazy) ... 15
cheese flavored:
(Cheese Nips) ... 5
(Cheese Tid-Bits) ... 4
(Cheez-It) ... 6
(Che-zo) ... 5
(Keebler Cheese Wafers) ... 11
chicken flavored (Chicken In A Biskit) ... 10

ham flavored (Hamies) 12
matzo, 1 sheet, as packaged:
(Goodman's Square) 110
(Goodman's Tea) 75
(Horowitz-Margareten Oven Crisp) 133
(Manischewitz Regular) 109
(Manischewitz Egg) 132
(Manischewitz Egg 'N Onion) 113
(Manischewitz Tasteas) 116
(Manischewitz Thin Teas) 111
(Manischewitz Whole Wheat) 124
melba toast, see "toasts and toasted crackers," below
onion flavored (Nabisco French Onion) 11
onion flavored (Onion Funion) 16
oyster:
(Dandy) 3
(Keebler) 3
(Oysterettes) 3
(Sunshine) 4
potato flavored (Chippers) 14
potato flavored (Potato Piffles) 17
rye (Keebler Rye Toast) 18
saltines, soda and water crackers:
(Crown Pilot) 73
(Keebler Export Sodas) 25
(Jacob's Biscuits for Cheese) 35
(Jacob's English Cream) 110
(Keebler Salt-Free) 14
(Keebler Saltines) 14
(Keebler Sea Toast) 61
(Keebler Whole Wheat Sea Toast) 58
(Krispy) 12
(Premium) 12
(Royal Lunch) 55
sesame (Keebler Sesame Bread Wafers) 16
sesame (Meal Mates) 22
sesame (Sesame Sillys) 16
sesame-cheese flavored (Sunshine Sesame Cheese Snacks) 16
(Sociables) 10
toasts and toasted crackers:
(Dutch Rusk) 61
(Holland Rusk) 38
(Keebler Party Toasts) 15

(Nabisco Zwieback) 31
(Old London Melba Toast Rounds) 9
(Old London Garlic Melba Toast Rounds) 9
(Old London Pumpernickel Melba Toast) 16
(Old London Rye Melba Toast) 16
(Old London Salty Rye Melba Toast Rounds) 8
(Old London Sesame Melba Toast Rounds) 11
(Old London Wheat Melba Toast) 16
(Old London White Melba Toast) 16
(Old London White Melba Toast Rounds) 9
(Sunshine Toasted Wafers) 10
(Sunshine Zwieback) 30
(Uneeda Biscuit) 22
tomato-onion flavored (Sunshine Tomato-Onion) 15
(Triangle Thins) 8
wheat (Keebler Wheat Toast) 15
wheat (Nabisco Wheat Thins) 9
wheat, shredded (Triscuit Wafers) 22

CRACKER SANDWICHES, 1 piece, as packaged

CALORIES

cheese crackers:
w/cheese filling (Nabisco) 34
w/cheese filling (Wise Cheese-N-Cheese) 32
w/peanut butter filling (Nabisco) 38
w/peanut butter filling (O-So-Gud) 36
w/peanut butter filling (Wise Peanut Butter Cheese) 34
rye crackers, w/cheese filling (Nabisco Cheese on Rye) 35
toasted crackers, w/peanut butter filling (Wise Peanut Butter Toast) ...33
waffle crackers, w/cheese filling (Cheez Waffies) 22
waffle crackers, w/blue cheese filling (Cheesewich) 22
waffle crackers, w/cheddar cheese filling (Cheesewich) 22

CRUMBS, MEAL & STUFFINGS

CALORIES

crumbs:
bread (Old London), 1 tbsp. 21
bread (Wonder), 1 cup 94
bread (Wonder), 4 oz. 431

crumbs, continued

bread, flavored (La Rosa), 1 cup 435
bread, flavored (La Rosa), 4 oz. 437
cracker, salted (Nabisco), 1 cup 308
cracker, salted (Nabisco), 4 oz. 411
cracker, unsalted (Nabisco), 1 cup 318
cracker, unsalted (Nabisco), 4 oz. 424
graham cracker (Nabisco), 1 cup 428
graham cracker (Nabisco), 4 oz. 466

meal:

corn, see "Flour," below
cracker (Keebler), 1 cup 449
cracker (Keebler), 4 oz. 422
graham cracker (Keebler), 1 cup 470
graham cracker (Keebler), 4 oz. 492
matzo (Horowitz-Margareten), 4 oz. 440
matzo (Manischewitz), 1 cup 438
matzo (Manischewitz), 4 oz. 437

stuffing:

bread, cubes (Pepperidge Farm), 1 cup 177
bread, cubes (Pepperidge Farm), 4 oz. 438
bread, herb seasoned (Pepperidge Farm), 1 cup 212
bread, herb seasoned (Pepperidge Farm), 4 oz. 425
cornbread (Pepperidge Farm), 1 cup 175
cornbread (Pepperidge Farm), 4 oz. 446

SEASONED COATING MIXES

CALORIES

(Shake 'n Bake—for chicken), 1 envelope 330
(Shake 'n Bake—for fish), 1 envelope 260

FLOUR, 1 cup

CALORIES

all purpose (Aunt Jemima) 449
cake* (Swans Down) 370
cake, self-rising (Presto) 380
cake, self-rising* (Swans Down) 350
cornmeal, self-rising (Aunt Jemima) 485
tortilla (Quaker Masa Harina) 404

* *Sifted*

BAKING POWDER, 1 teaspoon

	CALORIES
(Calumet)	2
(Royal)	4

CEREALS, PANCAKES AND WAFFLES

2

CEREAL, READY-TO-EAT, 1 cup, except as noted

See also "Cereal, Cooked"

	CALORIES
bran:	
(Kellogg's All-Bran)	192
(Kellogg's 40% Bran Flakes)	139
(Nabisco 100% Bran Flakes)	150
(Post 40% Bran Flakes)	134
w/prunes (Post Bran & Prune Flakes)	120
w/raisins (General Mills Bran & Raisin Flakes)	126
w/raisins (Kellogg's Raisin Bran)	200
w/sugar coated raisins (Post Raisin Bran)	178
w/wheat germ (Kellogg's Bran Buds)	196
corn:	
(General Mills Country Corn Flakes)	81
(General Mills Kix)	75
(Kellogg's Corn Flakes)	79
(Post Toasties Corn Flakes)	110
w/blueberries (Post Corn Flakes & Blueberries)	110
w/strawberries (Post Corn Flakes & Strawberries)	110
presweetened (Kellogg's Sugar Frosted Flakes)	143
presweetened (Kellogg's Sugar Pops)	110
presweetened (Post Honeycomb Sweet Crisp Corn)	83
presweetened (Post Sugar Sparkled Flakes)	147
cocoa flavored, presweetened (General Mills Cocoa Puffs)	107
fruit flavored, presweetened (General Mills Trix)	112
corn-oats, presweetened (General Mills Sugar Sparkled Twinkles)	112
corn-oats, presweetened (Quaker Cap'n Crunch)	163
corn-oats, presweetened (Quaker Quisp)	103

oats:
(General Mills Cheerios) 112
(Kellogg's OK's) 83
(Post Alpha-Bits) 110
(Post Crispy Critters) 110
(Post Fortified Oat Flakes) 165
(Quaker Life) 161
w/marshmallow bits (General Mills Lucky Charms) 110
presweetened (General Mills Frosty O's) 111
presweetened (General Mills Sugar Jets) 111
caramel flavored, presweetened (Kellogg's Stars) 110
fruit flavored, presweetened (Kellogg's Froot Loops) 114
rice:
(Kellogg's Rice Krispies) 106
(Quaker Puffed Rice) 45
presweetened (Kellogg's Puffa Puffa Rice) 120
presweetened (Nabisco Rice Honeys) 151
presweetened (Post Sugar Sparkled Rice Krinkles) 127
cocoa flavored, presweetened (Kellogg's Cocoa Krispies) 113
wheat:
(General Mills Total) 108
(General Mills Wheat Stax) 81
(General Mills Wheaties) 108
(Kellogg's Krumbles) 140
(Kellogg's Pep Wheat Flakes) 106
(Kellogg's Shredded Wheat), 1 biscuit 63
(Nabisco Shredded Wheat), 1 biscuit 92
(Nabisco Spoon Size Shredded Wheat), 1 biscuit 4
(Post Grape Nuts Flakes) 150
(Quaker Puffed Wheat) 38
(Quaker Shredded Wheat), 1 biscuit 69
presweetened (Kellogg's Sugar Crisp Puffed Wheat) 147
presweetened (Kellogg's Sugar Smacks) 110
presweetened (Nabisco Wheat Honeys) 152
miscellaneous mixed grains:
(Kellogg's Concentrate) 318
(Kellogg's Product 19) 106
(Kellogg's Special K) 70
(Nabisco Team Flakes) 83
(Post Grape Nuts) 400
presweetened (Kellogg's Apple Jacks) 112
presweetened (Quaker Quake) 118

CEREAL, COOKED*, 1 cup

See also "Cereal, Ready-to-Eat"

	CALORIES
corn meal mush (Quaker)	128
farina:	
(Cream of Wheat Instant)	133
(Cream of Wheat Mix 'N Eat)	140
(Cream of Wheat Quick)	133
(Cream of Wheat Regular)	133
(H-O)	168
(Quaker)	100
(Quaker**)	180
hominy grits (Quaker)	154
oats (H-O)	150
oats (Quaker)	161
oatmeal, instant (Quaker)	143
rice (Cream of Rice)	144
whole wheat, rolled (Quaker Pettijohns)	144

* *According to package directions*
** *According to package directions, with whole milk*

PANCAKES & WAFFLES

See also page 123

	CALORIES
pancakes:	
mix, prepared* (Aunt Jemima), 4"-diameter cake	61
mix, prepared* (Aunt Jemima Easy Pour), 4"-diameter cake	79
buckwheat, mix, prepared* (Aunt Jemima), 4"-diameter cake	64
buttermilk, mix, prepared* (Aunt Jemima), 4"-diameter cake	71
waffles:	
frozen (Aunt Jemima), 1 double waffle, as packaged	116
mix, prepared* (Aunt Jemima), 4½"-square waffle	175
mix, prepared* (Aunt Jemima Easy Pour), 4½"-square waffle	191
buckwheat, mix, prepared* (Aunt Jemima), 4½"-square waffle	181
buttermilk, mix, prepared* (Aunt Jemima), 4½"-square waffle	154

* *According to package directions*

FRUITS AND FRUIT DRINKS 3

FRUITS, ½ cup, except as noted

See also page 127

	CALORIES
apples and apricots, mixed, in jars (Mott's Fruit Treats)	104
apples and cherries, mixed, in jars (Mott's Fruit Treats)	109
apples and pineapple, mixed, in jars (Mott's Fruit Treats)	127
apples and raspberries, mixed, in jars (Mott's Fruit Treats)	111
apples and strawberries, mixed, in jars (Mott's Fruit Treats)	104
applesauce, in jars (Mott's)	105
apricots, dried (Sunsweet)	224
cherries, Bing, frozen (Birds Eye)	124
cherries, maraschino, bottled (Vita), 1 cherry	20
cranberry sauce, jellied, canned (Ocean Spray), 1 oz.	46
cranberry sauce, whole, canned (Ocean Spray), 1 oz.	48
dates, chopped (Dromedary), 4 oz.	397
dates, diced (Bordo), 4 oz.	330
dates, pitted (Bordo), 4 oz.	331
dates, pitted (Dromedary), 4 oz.	376
fruit cocktail, canned (Dole)	72
fruit salad,* fresh, dairy-packed (Kraft)	48
fruits and peels, glazed (Liberty), 4 oz.	388
grapefruit sections,* fresh, dairy-packed (Kraft)	43
melon balls, frozen (Birds Eye), ½ pkg.	72
mixed fruit, frozen (Birds Eye), ½ pkg.	186
orange sections,* fresh, dairy-packed (Kraft)	52
peaches:	
canned (Heart's Delight Elberta Freestone)	127
canned (Heart's Delight Yellow Cling)	99
canned (Hunt's Cling)	96
dried (Sunsweet)	216
spiced, canned (Hunt's), 1 peach	175
peaches and strawberries, frozen (Birds Eye)	81

fruits, continued

pears, dried (Sunsweet) 208
pineapple:
  chunks, in juice, canned (Dole) 64
  chunks, in syrup, canned (Dole—#2 or #2½ size can) 84
  chunks, frozen (Dole) 92
  crushed, in juice, canned (Dole) 64
  crushed, in syrup, canned (Dole—buffet or #1 size can) 94
  crushed, in syrup, canned (Dole—#2 or #2½ size can) 84
  sliced, in juice, canned (Dole), 1 slice* 32
  sliced, in syrup, canned (Dole—#1 or #2 size can), 1 slice* 42
  sliced, in syrup, canned (Dole—#1¼ size can), 1 slice* 76
  sliced, in syrup, canned (Dole—#2½ size can), 1 slice* 79
  spears, canned (Dole), 2 spears* 52
  tidbits, canned (Dole—buffet or #2 size can) 94
prunes, dried (Sunsweet) 272
prunes, stewed, canned (Heart's Delight) 210
prunes, stewed, canned (Sunsweet) 195
raisins, seedless (Sun Maid) 214
raspberries, red, frozen (Birds Eye Quick Thaw) 129
raspberries, red, frozen (Seabrook Farms) 120
rhubarb, frozen (Birds Eye) 138
strawberries, halves, frozen (Birds Eye) 162
strawberries, sliced, frozen (Seabrook Farms) 140
strawberries, whole, frozen (Birds Eye) 101

* *Drained of liquid*

FRUIT JUICES, 6-ounce glass, except as noted

See also "Fruit & Fruit-Flavored Drinks" and pages 129-130

CALORIES

apple, canned (Heinz) 75
apple, canned (Mott's) 84
apricot nectar, canned (Cal Fame) 194
apricot nectar, canned (Heart's Delight) 104
apricot nectar, canned (Heinz) 88
cranberry cocktail, bottled (Ocean Spray) 124
cranberry-apple, bottled (Cranapple) 120
fig, bottled (RealFig) 132
grape:
  bottled (Welch's) 128

canned (Heinz) 122
frozen, reconstituted* (Minute Maid) 99
frozen, reconstituted* (Snow Crop) 99
frozen, reconstituted* (Welch's) 90
grapefruit:
fresh, dairy-packed (Tropicana) 75
canned (Heinz) 68
frozen, reconstituted* (Birds Eye) 72
frozen, reconstituted* (Minute Maid) 75
frozen, reconstituted* (Snow Crop) 75
lemon, bottled (ReaLemon), 2 tbsp. 8
lemon, frozen, reconstituted* (Minute Maid), 2 tbsp. 7
lemon, frozen, reconstituted* (Snow Crop), 2 tbsp. 7
lime, bottled (ReaLime), 2 tbsp. 12
lime, sweetened, bottled (Holland House), 2 tbsp. 45
lime, sweetened, bottled (Rose's), 2 tbsp. 49
orange:
fresh, dairy-packed (Borden's) 96
fresh, dairy-packed (Sealtest) 96
fresh, dairy-packed (Tropicana) 83
canned (Heinz) 75
frozen, reconstituted* (Birds Eye) 77
frozen, reconstituted* (Minute Maid) 90
frozen, reconstituted* (Snow Crop) 90
imitation, frozen, prepared* (Awake) 77
orange-grapefruit, frozen, reconstituted* (Birds Eye) 72
orange-grapefruit, frozen, reconstituted* (Minute Maid) 76
orange-grapefruit, frozen, reconstituted* (Snow Crop) 76
peach nectar, canned (Heart's Delight) 89
pear nectar, canned (Heart's Delight) 95
pineapple, canned (Dole) 110
pineapple, canned (Heinz) 94
pineapple, frozen, reconstituted* (Dole) 101
pineapple-grapefruit, frozen, reconstituted* (Dole) 77
pineapple-orange, frozen, reconstituted* (Dole) 77
prune, bottled or canned (RealPrune) 144
prune, bottled or canned (Sunsweet) 128
prune, canned (Heinz) 130
prune, canned (Lady Betty) 123
tangerine, frozen, reconstituted* (Minute Maid) 85
tangerine, frozen, reconstituted* (Snow Crop) 85

* *According to package directions*

FRUIT & FRUIT-FLAVORED DRINKS, 8-ounce glass

See also "Fruit Juices" and pages 129-130

	CALORIES
apple, canned (Hi-C)	116
apple-grape, canned (Welch's)	124
cherry, canned (Hi-C)	122
cranberry-orange, mix, prepared* (Knox Gelatine)	79
grape, canned (Cal Fame)	128
grape, canned (Hi-C)	117
grape, w/lemon, frozen, reconstituted* (Welch's)	120
grapeade, canned (Welchade)	120
grapeade, dairy-packed (Sealtest)	126
grapefruit, dairy-packed (Sealtest)	121
grapefruit, pink, mix, prepared* (Start)	120
lemon-lime, canned (Cal Fame)	128
lemon-orange, canned (Cal Fame)	128
lemonade:	
dairy-packed (Borden's)	109
dairy-packed (Sealtest)	110
frozen, reconstituted* (Birds Eye)	98
frozen, reconstituted* (Minute Maid)	98
frozen, reconstituted* (ReaLemon)	104
frozen, reconstituted* (Snow Crop)	98
mix, prepared* (Twist)	82
mix, prepared* (Wyler's)	81
pink, frozen, reconstituted* (Birds Eye)	102
pink, frozen, reconstituted* (ReaLemon)	104
limeade, frozen, reconstituted* (Birds Eye)	102
limeade, frozen, reconstituted* (Minute Maid)	100
limeade, frozen, reconstituted* (ReaLemon)	104
mixed flavors, canned (Juicidrink)	136
mixed flavors, canned (Mott's A.M.)	122
mixed flavors, canned (Mott's P.M.)	122
orange:	
canned (Hi-C)	118
dairy-packed (Sealtest)	111
mix, prepared* (Knox Gelatine)	79
mix, prepared* (Start)	120
mix, prepared* (Tang)	118
mix, prepared* (Wyler's)	71

orangeade, dairy-packed (Sealtest) 124
orangeade, frozen, reconstituted* (Minute Maid) 125
orangeade, mix, prepared* (Twist) 92
orange-pineapple, canned (Hi-C) 117
orange-pineapple, mix, prepared* (Start) 120
pineapple-grapefruit, canned (Dole) 124
pineapple-grapefruit, canned (Hi-C) 125
pineapple-grapefruit, mix, prepared* (Start) 120
pineapple-grapefruit, mix, prepared* (Wyler's) 94
pineapple-orange, canned (Cal Fame) 128
pineapple-pink grapefruit, canned (Dole) 124
punch:
  canned (Hi-C) 130
  canned (Welch's) 126
  cherry-lemon, frozen, reconstituted* (ReaLemon) 112
  grape, canned (Hawaiian Punch) 108
  grape-lemon, frozen, reconstituted* (ReaLemon) 112
  orange, canned (Hawaiian Punch) 111
  pineapple-raspberry, frozen, reconstituted* (ReaLemon) 112
  raspberry-lemon, frozen, reconstituted* (ReaLemon) 112
  red, canned (Hawaiian Punch) 107
  strawberry-lemon, frozen, reconstituted* (ReaLemon) 112
  yellow, canned (Hawaiian Punch) 115

* *According to package directions*

MILK, CREAM AND RELATED PRODUCTS 4

MILK, 8-ounce glass, except as noted

See also "Milk Beverages, Flavored"

buttermilk:
- (Foremost)* 110
- 0.1% fat (Borden's) 83
- 0.5% fat (Borden's) 90
- 0.5% fat (Meadow Gold) 105
- 1% fat (Borden's) 100
- 1% fat (Sealtest) 100
- 1.5% fat (Borden's) 110
- 2% fat (Borden's) 122
- 3.5% fat (Borden's) 151

condensed, sweetened, canned (Borden's Dime Brand), ½ cup 504
condensed, sweetened, canned (Borden's Eagle Brand), ½ cup 500
condensed, sweetened, canned (Borden's Magnolia Brand), ½ cup 504
dry, nonfat, reconstituted** (Borden's) 82
dry, nonfat, reconstituted** (Carnation) 82
dry, nonfat, reconstituted** (Foremost Milkman) 97
dry, nonfat, reconstituted** (Pet Instant) 81
evaporated, canned (Borden's) 345
evaporated, canned (Carnation) 348
half and half, see "Cream," page 19
skim:
- (Foremost Profile)* 90
- (Foremost So-Lo)* 133
- (Viva)* 137
- 0.1% fat (Borden's) 81
- 0.1% fat (Sealtest) 81
- 0.5% fat (Meadow Gold) 87
- 2% fat (Borden's Hi Protein) 138

fortified, 0.1% fat (Borden's) 81
fortified, 0.1% fat (Gail Borden) 81
fortified, 1% fat (Sealtest Light 'n Lively) 116
fortified, 1.5% fat (Sealtest n-r-g) 127
fortified, 1.75% fat (Borden's Lifeline) 132
fortified, 2% fat (Sealtest Vita Lure) 137
modified, 0.1% fat (Borden's) 98
modified, 0.5% fat (Borden's) 107
modified, 2% fat (Borden's) 139
whole:
(Foremost)* 154
3.3% fat (Meadow Gold) 166
3.5% fat (Borden's) 151
3.5% fat (Sealtest) 151
3.7% fat (Borden's Cream Line) 159
3.7% fat (Sealtest) 159
3.8% fat (Borden's) 160
fortified, 3.5% fat (Sealtest Multivitamin) 151
fortified, 3.7% fat (Gail Borden) 159

* *Information on fat content unavailable*
** *According to package directions*

MILK BEVERAGES, FLAVORED, 8-ounce glass

See also "Eggnog, Nonalcoholic" and page 168

CALORIES

cherry-vanilla, mix, prepared* (Borden's Frosted Shake) 185
cherry-vanilla, w/ice cream, canned (Borden's Milk Shake) 291
chocolate:
drink, 1% fat, dairy-packed (Sealtest) 154
drink, 2% fat, dairy-packed (Borden's Dutch Chocolate) 181
drink, 2% fat, dairy-packed (Meadow Gold) 185
drink, canned (Borden's Dutch Chocolate) 213
milk, 2% fat, dairy-packed (Borden's Dutch Chocolate) 122
milk, 3.3% fat, dairy-packed (Meadow Gold) 200
milk, 3.5% fat, dairy-packed (Borden's Dutch Chocolate) 210
milk, 3.5% fat, dairy-packed (Sealtest) 205
mix, prepared* (Borden's Frosted Shake) 221
mix, prepared** (Borden's Hemo) 235
mix, prepared** (Borden's Instant Dutch Chocolate) 246
mix, prepared† (Carnation Instant Breakfast) 290

chocolate, continued

mix, prepared† (Foremost Instant Breakfast) 290
mix, prepared* (Great Shakes) 259
mix, prepared† (Hershey's Hot Chocolate) 275
mix, prepared** (Nestlé's Quik) 215
mix, prepared† (Nestlé's Quik Shake) 255
w/ice cream, canned (Borden's Milk Shake) 291

chocolate fudge, mix, prepared† (Foremost Instant Breakfast) 290
chocolate fudge, mix, prepared* (Great Shakes) 259
chocolate fudge, w/ice cream, canned (Borden's Milk Shake) 291
chocolate malted, mix, prepared** (Borden's Instant Malted) 236
chocolate malted, mix, prepared† (Nestlé's Quik Shake) 263
chocolate marshmallow, w/ice cream, canned (Borden's Milk Shake) .. 291

cocoa:

mix, prepared† (Hershey's Instant) 264
mix, prepared† (Nestlé's Deluxe) 245
mix, prepared* (Royal Instant) 110
mix, prepared† (Royal Instant) 270

coffee, mix, prepared† (Foremost Instant Breakfast) 290
coffee, w/ice cream, canned (Borden's Milk Shake) 291
malted, mix, prepared** (Borden's Instant Malted) 239
mocha, w/ice cream, canned (Borden's Milk Shake) 291

strawberry:

mix, prepared* (Borden's Frosted Shake) 219
mix, prepared† (Carnation Instant Breakfast) 290
mix, prepared† (Foremost Instant Breakfast) 290
mix, prepared* (Great Shakes) 259
mix, prepared** (Nestlé's Quik) 221
mix, prepared† (Nestlé's Quik Shake) 265
w/ice cream, canned (Borden's Milk Shake) 291

vanilla:

mix, prepared* (Borden's Frosted Shake) 160
mix, prepared† (Carnation Instant Breakfast) 290
mix, prepared† (Foremost Instant Breakfast) 290
mix, prepared* (Great Shakes) 259
mix, prepared† (Nestlé's Quik Shake) 270
w/ice cream, canned (Borden's Milk Shake) 291

* *According to package directions*
** *2 heaping teaspoons in an 8-ounce glass of whole fresh milk*
† *1 ounce in an 8-ounce glass of whole fresh milk*

CREAM, 1 tablespoon

See also "Creamers, Non-Dairy" and "Sour Cream"

	CALORIES
half and half:	
(Foremost)*	21
10.5% fat (Borden's)	19
10.5% fat (Sealtest)	19
12% fat (Meadow Gold)	30
12% fat (Sealtest)	21
heavy, whipping** (Borden's)	52
heavy, whipping** (Foremost)	54
heavy, whipping** (Meadow Gold)	50
heavy, whipping** (Sealtest)	52
light, table or coffee, 18% fat (Borden's)	28
light, table or coffee, 18% fat (Sealtest)	28
light, table or coffee, 20% fat (Foremost)	31
light, table or coffee, 25% fat (Sealtest)	37
medium, whipping** (Borden's)	44
medium, whipping** (Sealtest)	44
whipped, see "Dessert Topping," page 86	

* *Information on fat content unavailable*
** *Unwhipped (volume approximately double when whipped)*

CREAMERS, NON-DAIRY, 1 teaspoon

	CALORIES
(Cremora)	11
(Coffee-mate)	11
half and half (Meadow Gold)	9
half and half (Reddi-Wip Coffee White)	7
half and half (Sta-Wip Coffee White)	7
whipped, see "Dessert Toppings," page 86	

SOUR CREAM, 1 tablespoon

	CALORIES
plain (Borden's)	29
plain (Foremost)	31
plain (Sealtest)	29

sour cream, continued

half and half (Borden's) 20
imitation (Borden's Zesty-Sour) 25

YOGURT, 8-ounce cup

See also page 126

	CALORIES
plain (Borden's Swiss Style)	167
plain (Dannon)	130
flavored:	
apple, spiced (Borden's Swiss Style)	270
apricot (Borden's Swiss Style)	270
apricot (Dannon)	260
blueberry (Borden's Swiss Style)	270
blueberry (Dannon)	260
boysenberry (Borden's Swiss Style)	270
cherry (Borden's Swiss Style)	270
coffee (Borden's Swiss Style)	270
coffee (Dannon)	200
orange, mandarin (Borden's Swiss Style)	270
pear (Borden's Swiss Style)	270
pineapple-orange (Dannon)	260
prune (Borden's Swiss Style)	270
prune (Dannon)	260
raspberry (Borden's Swiss Style)	270
raspberry (Dannon)	260
strawberry (Borden's Swiss Style)	270
strawberry (Dannon)	260
vanilla (Borden's Swiss Style)	270
vanilla (Dannon)	200

EGGNOG, NONALCOHOLIC, 8-ounce glass

	CALORIES
4.7% fat, canned (Borden's)	263
6% fat, canned (Borden's)	302
6% fat, dairy-packed (Meadow Gold)	327
6.8% fat, dairy-packed (Sealtest)	354
8% fat, canned (Borden's)	342
8.8% fat, dairy-packed (Sealtest)	390

CHEESE AND CHEESE PRODUCTS 5

CHEESE, 1 ounce, except as noted

See also "Cheese Food," "Cheese Spreads," etc., and page 124

Unless noted otherwise, the figure listed for any cheese below applies to all of the forms in which it may be packaged—sliced, in bars, loaves, wedges, etc. For example, Kraft's Old English cheese is packaged in loaves and slices, but in either form it contains the same 105 calories per ounce. However, do be careful not to confuse cheese with a "cheese spread" or "cheese food" that bears the same or a similar name. For instance, in addition to Old English cheese, you can also buy Old English cheese *spread* which has 97 calories per ounce. Generally, it isn't hard to differentiate between cheese and cheese spreads, but cheese foods sometimes pose a problem (especially when they're packaged in slices). Check the label if you're confused about a product; if it is either a cheese spread or cheese food, the label will say so.

	CALORIES
American:	
(Borden's)	104
(Borden's Made in Wisconsin)	104
(Kraft)	105
(Kraft Old English)	105
("Vera-Sharp")	104
w/brick (Kraft)	101
w/Monterey (Kraft)	101
w/Muenster (Kraft)	100
asiago (Frigo)	113
blue:	
(Borden's Blufort Brand), 1¼-oz. portion	131
(Borden's Danish)	105
(Borden's Flora Danica)	105
(Frigo)	99
(Kraft)	99

natural (Dorman's Endeco) ... 90
natural (Kraft) ... 100
processed (Kraft) ... 102
Neufchâtel, see "Cream & Neufchâtel Cheese," page 24
nuworld (Kraft) ... 104
Parmesan (Frigo) ... 107
Parmesan (Kraft) ... 107
Parmesan, grated, see "Grated Cheese," page 24
Pepato (Frigo) ... 110
pimento (Borden's) ... 104
pimento (Borden's Made in Wisconsin) ... 104
pimento-American (Kraft) ... 104
pizza:
(Borden's) ... 85
(Frigo) ... 73
(Kraft) ... 73
shredded (Kraft) ... 86
Port DuSalut (Kraft) ... 100
Prim-ost (Kraft) ... 134
Provolone (Borden's) ... 93
Provolone (Frigo) ... 99
Provolone (Kraft) ... 99
Ricotta, moist (Borden's) ... 42
Romano (Borden's Italian Pecorino) ... 114
Romano (Frigo) ... 110
Romano (Kraft) ... 110
Romano, grated, see "Grated Cheese," page 24
Roquefort (Borden's Napoleon Brand) ... 107
Roquefort (Kraft) ... 105
Sap Sago (Kraft) ... 76
Sardo Romano (Kraft) ... 110
Scamorze (Frigo) ... 79
Scamorze (Kraft) ... 100
Swiss:
natural (Borden's) ... 104
natural (Borden's Finland Imported) ... 104
natural (Borden's Switzerland Imported) ... 104
natural (Dorman's Endeco) ... 90
natural (Kraft) ... 104
processed (Borden's) ... 100
processed (Borden's Made in Wisconsin) ... 100
processed (Borden's Milkboy Brand) ... 96
processed (Kraft—loaf) ... 93

Swiss cheese, continued

processed (Kraft—slices) 95
hickory smoke flavored, processed (Borden's) 103
hickory smoke flavored, processed (Dorman's Endeco) 100
w/American, processed (Kraft) 99
w/Muenster, processed (Kraft) 98
washed curd (Kraft) 108

GRATED CHEESE, 1 tablespoon

See also page 124

CALORIES

American (Borden's) 30
Parmesan (Buitoni) 23
Parmesan (Frigo) 27
Parmesan (Kraft) 27
Parmesan (La Rosa) 34
Parmesan-Romano (Borden's) 30
Romano (Buitoni) 21
Romano (Frigo) 29
Romano (Kraft) 26

CREAM & NEUFCHATEL CHEESE, 1 ounce

See also "Cheese Spreads," "Dips, Ready-to-Eat" and page 124

CALORIES

cream cheese, foil wrapped and/or in jars:
plain (Borden's) 96
plain (Kraft) 98
w/bacon and horseradish (Kraft) 91
w/chive (Borden's) 96
w/chive (Kraft) 84
w/dates and nuts (Borden's) 96
w/olive and pimento (Kraft) 85
w/pimento (Borden's) 74
w/pimento (Kraft) 85
w/pineapple (Kraft) 87
w/relish (Kraft) 88
w/Roquefort (Kraft) 80

cream cheese, whipped, in foil dishes:

plain (Kraft)	101
w/bacon and horseradish (Kraft)	95
w/blue (Kraft)	99
w/chive (Kraft)	92
w/herbs and spices (Kraft Catalina)	94
w/onion (Kraft)	93
w/pimento (Kraft)	91
w/Roquefort (Kraft)	99

Neufchâtel:

(Borden's Eagle Brand)	73
(Kraft)	69

Neufchâtel spreads, in foil dishes and/or jars:

w/bacon and horseradish (Kraft Party Snack)	74
w/blue cheese (Kraft Roka Blue)	80
w/chipped beef (Kraft Party Snack)	67
w/chive (Kraft Party Snack)	69
w/clam (Kraft Party Snack)	67
w/olive and pimento (Kraft)	70
w/onion soup (Kraft Party Snack)	66
w/pimento (Kraft)	67
w/pimento (Kraft Party Snack)	67
w/pineapple (Borden's)	81
w/pineapple (Kraft)	70
w/relish (Kraft)	71

CHEESE SPREADS*, 1 ounce, except as noted

See also "Cream & Neufchâtel Cheese," "Cheese Food," page 125

	CALORIES
American:	
(Kraft)	77
(Kraft Old English)	97
(Snack Mate)	90
("Vera-Sharp")	80
bacon (Borden's Cheese 'N Bacon)	80
bacon (Kraft)	92
blue (Borden's Blue Brand)	82
blue (Wispride)	95
(Borden's Chateau)	92
cheddar (Snack Mate)	84

cheese spreads, continued

cheddar (Wispride Sharp)	97
(Cheez Whiz)	76
garlic (Kraft)	86
hickory smoke flavored (Borden's)	80
hickory smoke flavored (Smokelle)	90
(Kraft Sharpie)	90
(Laughing Cow)	74
(Laughing Cow—cubes), 1 cube	13
Limburger (Mohawk Valley)	70
Limburger (Moose Brand)	70
pimento:	
(Cheez Whiz Pimento)	76
(Kraft)	77
(Phenix)	80
(Snack Mate)	90
(Velveeta Pimento)	84
(Velveeta)	84
imitation (Kraft Tasty Loaf)	48

* *See "Cheese," page 21, to be certain you don't confuse a cheese spread with cheese or a cheese food*

CHEESE FOOD*, 1 ounce

See also "Cheese," "Cheese Spreads" and page 125

	CALORIES
American (Kraft)	77
bacon (Kraft)	93
bacon (Kraft Cheez'n Bacon)	101
garlic (Kraft)	93
hickory smoke flavored (Smokelle)	93
Jalapeno pepper (Kraft)	93
(Kraft Munst-ett)	101
(Kraft Super Blend)	92
(Kraft Super Blend with Caraway)	94
pimento (Velveeta Pimento)	90
pizza (Kraft Pizzalone)	90
sharp (Kraft)	97
sharp (Nippy Brand)	93
Swiss (Kraft)	91

* *See "Cheese," page 21, to be certain you don't confuse a cheese food with cheese or a cheese spread*

COTTAGE CHEESE, ½ cup

See also page 124

	CALORIES
creamed:	
(Borden's)	120
(Foremost)	106
(Meadow Gold)	117
(Sealtest)	107
w/chives (Borden's)	117
w/pineapple (Borden's)	107
w/pineapple (Sealtest)	101
w/vegetable salad (Borden's)	119
w/vegetable salad (Sealtest's Spring Garden Salad)	105
creamed partially (Meadow Gold)	102
uncreamed (Borden's)	98
uncreamed (Kraft)	103
uncreamed (Sealtest)	90

SOUPS, BROTHS AND CHOWDERS

6

SOUPS, BROTHS & CHOWDERS, 8-ounce cup

See also page 131

Bear in mind that you can considerably reduce the number of calories in a cream soup prepared at home by using skim milk or water in place of whole milk. If you use skim milk, a cup of the prepared soup will contain 25 to 40 fewer calories (depending on the fat content of the milk) than you see listed here; if you substitute water, the same soup will contain about 80 less calories!

	CALORIES
alphabet, mix, prepared* (Golden Grain)	55
alphabet vegetable, mix, prepared* (Lipton)	68
asparagus, cream of, canned, prepared** (Campbell's)	165
bean:	
canned (Manischewitz)	112
mix, prepared* (Wyler's)	96
w/bacon, canned, prepared* (Campbell's)	173
w/hot dogs, canned, prepared* (Campbell's)	168
w/smoked pork, canned, prepared* (Heinz)	157
bean, black, canned, prepared* (Campbell's)	95
bean, black, canned (Crosse & Blackwell)	118
bean, lima, canned (Manischewitz)	93
beef:	
canned, prepared* (Campbell's)	106
bouillon, see "bouillon, beef," page 29	
broth, see "broth, beef," page 29	
consommé, see "consommé, beef," page 30	
w/barley, canned (Manischewitz)	83
w/cabbage, canned (Manischewitz)	62
w/noodles, canned, prepared* (Campbell's)	69
w/noodles, canned, prepared* (Heinz)	74
w/noodles, canned (Manischewitz)	64

w/noodles, mix, prepared* (Knorr) .60
w/noodles, mix, prepared* (Lipton) .67
w/noodles, mix, prepared* (Wyler's) .49
w/vegetables, canned (Manischewitz) .59
borscht, bottled (Manischewitz) .72
borscht, bottled (Mother's) .90
borscht, bottled (Rokeach) .75
borscht, bottled, egg-enriched (Mother's) .124
bouillon:
beef, 1 cube, prepared* (Herb-Ox) .7
beef, 1 cube, prepared* (Knorr Swiss) .17
beef, 1 cube, prepared* (Maggi) .7
beef, 1 cube, prepared* (Wyler's) .7
beef, 1 tsp. instant, prepared* (Maggi) .7
beef, 1 tsp. instant, prepared* (Wyler's) .4
chicken, 1 cube, prepared* (Herb-Ox) .7
chicken, 1 cube, prepared* (Knorr Swiss) .17
chicken, 1 cube, prepared* (Maggi) .8
chicken, 1 cube, prepared* (Wyler's) .6
chicken, 1 tsp. instant, prepared* (Maggi) .8
chicken, 1 tsp. instant, prepared* (Wyler's) .4
vegetable, 1 cube, prepared* (Herb-Ox) .7
vegetable, 1 cube, prepared* (Wyler's) .8
broth:
beef, canned, prepared* (Campbell's) .26
beef, canned (College Inn) .11
chicken, canned, prepared* (Campbell's) .43
chicken, canned (College Inn) .32
chicken, canned (Richardson & Robbins) .17
chicken, w/noodles, canned (College Inn) .45
chicken, w/rice, canned (College Inn) .45
chicken, w/rice, canned (Richardson & Robbins) .45
celery, cream of, canned, prepared** (Campbell's) .159
celery, cream of, canned, prepared** (Heinz) .181
cheddar cheese, canned, prepared* (Campbell's) .152
chicken:
bouillon, see "bouillon, chicken," above
broth, see "broth, chicken," above
consommé, see "consommé, chicken," page 30
cream of, canned, prepared** (Campbell's) .171
cream of, canned, prepared** (Heinz) .173
gumbo, canned, prepared* (Campbell's) .58

chicken, continued

w/barley, canned, prepared* (Manischewitz) 83
w/dumplings, canned, prepared* (Campbell's) 99
w/kasha, canned, prepared* (Manischewitz) 41
w/noodle stars, canned, prepared* (Campbell's) 60
w/noodle stars, canned, prepared* (Heinz) 67
w/noodles, canned, prepared* (Campbell's) 66
w/noodles, canned, prepared* (Heinz) 75
w/noodles, canned, prepared* (Manischewitz) 46
w/noodles, mix, prepared* (Golden Grain) 34
w/noodles, mix, prepared* (Lipton) 54
w/noodles, mix, prepared* (Wyler's) 44
w/noodles and chicken chunks, mix, prepared* (Knorr) 60
w/noodles and chicken chunks, mix, prepared* (Wyler's) 47
w/noodles and diced chicken, mix, prepared* (Lipton) 66
w/rice, canned, prepared* (Campbell's) 51
w/rice, canned, prepared* (Heinz) 58
w/rice, canned, prepared* (Manischewitz) 48
w/rice, mix, prepared* (Lipton) 59
w/rice, mix, prepared* (Wyler's) 49
w/vegetables, canned, prepared* (Campbell's) 73
w/vegetables, canned, prepared* (Heinz) 85
w/vegetables, canned (Manischewitz) 55
w/vegetables, mix, prepared* (Lipton) 70

chili, w/beef, canned, prepared* (Campbell's) 164
chili, w/beef, canned, prepared* (Heinz) 161

chowder:

clam, Manhattan, canned, prepared* (Campbell's) 77
clam, Manhattan, canned, prepared* (Doxsee) 62
clam, Manhattan, canned, prepared* (Heinz) 74
clam, Manhattan, canned, prepared* (Howard Johnson's) 104
clam, Manhattan, canned (Crosse & Blackwell) 75
clam, New England, canned, prepared** (Doxsee) 139
clam, New England, canned, prepared** (Howard Johnson's) 160
clam, New England, canned, prepared** (Snow's) 147
clam, New England, canned (Crosse & Blackwell) 124
clam, New England, frozen, prepared** (Campbell's) 206
corn, canned, prepared** (Snow's) 154
fish, canned, prepared** (Snow's) 134

consommé:

beef, canned, prepared* (Campbell's) 33
beef, mix, prepared* (Knorr Swiss) 20
chicken, mix, prepared* (Knorr Swiss) 20

Madrilene, clear, canned (Crosse & Blackwell) 41
Madrilene, red, canned (Crosse & Blackwell) 41
oxtail, mix, prepared* (Knorr Swiss) 20
crab, canned (Crosse & Blackwell) 73
gazpacho, canned (Crosse & Blackwell) 74
leek, cream of, mix, prepared* (Knorr) 73
lentil, canned (La Rosa) 137
lentil, canned (Manischewitz) 166
lobster, cream of, canned (Crosse & Blackwell) 113
Madrilene, see "consommé, Madrilene," above
minestrone, canned, prepared* (Campbell's) 88
minestrone, canned (La Rosa) 116
minestrone, mix, prepared* (Golden Grain) 66
mushroom:
canned, prepared* (Campbell's) 80
mix, prepared* (Golden Grain) 95
bisque, canned (Crosse & Blackwell) 127
cream of, canned, prepared** (Campbell's) 217
cream of, canned, prepared** (Heinz) 201
cream of, mix, prepared** (Knorr) 116
cream of, mix, prepared** (Lipton) 92
cream of, mix, prepared** (Wyler's) 151
noodles, w/ground beef, canned, prepared* (Campbell's) 98
onion:
canned, prepared* (Campbell's) 44
canned (Crosse & Blackwell French) 57
mix, prepared* (Golden Grain) 33
mix, prepared* (Knorr) 45
mix, prepared* (Lipton) 35
mix, prepared* (Wyler's) 37
oyster stew, canned, prepared** (Campbell's) 146
oyster stew, frozen, prepared** (Campbell's) 196
pea:
green, canned, prepared* (Campbell's) 148
green, mix, prepared* (Golden Grain) 73
green, mix, prepared* (Knorr Swiss) 71
green, mix, prepared* (Lipton) 136
green, w/ham, frozen, prepared* (Campbell's) 130
split, canned (Manischewitz) 133
split, w/ham, canned, prepared* (Campbell's) 179
split, w/ham, canned, prepared* (Heinz) 150
pepper pot, canned, prepared* (Campbell's) 105
Petite Marmite, canned (Crosse & Blackwell) 41

potato, mix, prepared** (Lipton) 100
potato, cream of, canned, prepared** (Campbell's) 190
potato, cream of, frozen, prepared** (Campbell's) 185
potato, w/leek, mix, prepared** (Wyler's) 155
schav, bottled (Manischewitz) 11
schav, bottled (Rokeach) 12
schav, bottled, egg-enriched (Mother's) 24
Scotch broth, canned, prepared* (Campbell's) 90
Senegalese, canned (Crosse & Blackwell) 75
shrimp, cream of, canned (Crosse & Blackwell) 113
shrimp, cream of, frozen, prepared** (Campbell's) 230
tomato:
- canned, prepared* (Campbell's) 84
- canned, prepared* (Heinz) 87
- canned (Manischewitz) 61
- bisque, canned, prepared* (Campbell's) 126
- w/rice, canned, prepared* (Campbell's) 106
- w/rice, canned (Manischewitz) 78
- w/vegetables, mix, prepared* (Golden Grain) 86
- w/vegetables, mix, prepared* (Lipton) 69

tuna creole, canned (Crosse & Blackwell) 70
turkey, w/noodles, canned, prepared* (Campbell's) 75
turkey, w/noodles, canned, prepared* (Heinz) 83
turkey, w/noodles, mix, prepared* (Lipton) 74
turkey, w/vegetables, canned, prepared* (Campbell's) 78
vegetable:
- canned, prepared* (Campbell's) 83
- canned, prepared* (Campbell's Old-Fashioned) 74
- canned (Manischewitz) 63
- bouillon, see "bouillon, vegetable," page 29
- mix, prepared* (Knorr) 70
- mix, prepared* (Wyler's) 56
- w/beef, canned, prepared* (Campbell's) 81
- w/beef, canned, prepared* (Campbell's Stockpot) 96
- w/beef, canned, prepared* (Heinz) 66
- w/beef, frozen, prepared* (Campbell's Old-Fashioned) 79
- w/beef, mix, prepared* (Lipton) 53

vegetarian, canned, prepared* (Campbell's) 76
vegetarian, canned, prepared* (Heinz) 83

* *According to package directions, with water*
** *According to package directions, with whole fresh milk*

VEGETABLES AND VEGETABLE PRODUCTS

7

VEGETABLES, ½ cup, except as noted

See also page 133

	CALORIES
artichoke hearts, frozen (Birds Eye), 5-6 hearts*	22
asparagus:	
spears, frozen (Birds Eye), 5 spears*	23
spears, frozen (Seabrook Farms), 5 spears*	19
cuts, frozen (Birds Eye)	21
cuts and tips, frozen (Seabrook Farms)	16
cuts and tips, in Hollandaise sauce, frozen (Seabrook Farms)	84
bamboo shoots, canned (Chun King)	30
bean sprouts, canned (Chun King)	10
bean sprouts, canned (La Choy)	8
beans, baked, see "Beans, Baked" and "Beans, Baked-Style," page 37	
beans, butter, see "butterbeans," page 34	
beans, chili, in sauce, wo/meat, canned (Morton House)	149
beans, chili, spiced, Mexican style, canned (Gebhardt), 4 oz.**	92
beans, green:	
whole, canned (Comstock)	23
whole, frozen (Birds Eye)	23
whole, frozen (Birds Eye Italian)	23
cut, canned (Comstock)	23
cut, frozen (Birds Eye)	23
cut, frozen (Seabrook Farms)	18
cut, in jars (Lord Mott's)	20
French-style, canned (Comstock)	18
French-style, frozen (Birds Eye)	23
French-style, in jars (Lord Mott's)	20
French-style, w/almonds, frozen (Birds Eye)	51
French-style, w/mushrooms, frozen (Birds Eye)	26
French-style, in butter sauce, frozen (Birds Eye)	48
French-style, in mushroom sauce, frozen (Seabrook Farms)	100

beans, lima:
  baby, frozen (Birds Eye) 114
  baby, frozen (Seabrook Farms) 115
  Fordhook, frozen (Birds Eye) 96
  Fordhook, in butter sauce, frozen (Birds Eye) 117
  in cheese sauce, frozen (Seabrook Farms) 140
beans, pinto, cooked† (Uncle Ben's) 98
beans, refried, Mexican style, canned (Gebhardt), 4 oz.** 120
beans, wax, frozen (Birds Eye) 25
beans, wax, cut, canned (Comstock) 21
beans, wax, French-style, canned (Comstock) 21
beans, white, small, cooked† (Uncle Ben's) 88
beets:
  diced, canned (Comstock) 41
  sliced, in jars (Lord Mott's) 25
  Harvard, canned (Greenwood's) 54
  Harvard, in jars (Lord Mott's) 40
  pickled, canned (Greenwood's) 78
  pickled, in jars (Lord Mott's) 63
broccoli:
  spears, frozen (Birds Eye) 26
  chopped, frozen (Birds Eye) 27
  chopped, frozen (Seabrook Farms) 30
  spears, in butter sauce, frozen (Birds Eye) 58
  chopped, in cream sauce, frozen (Birds Eye) 118
Brussels sprouts, frozen (Birds Eye) 34
butterbeans, frozen (Birds Eye), ⅓ pkg. 123
butterbeans, frozen (Seabrook Farms) 102
cabbage, red, sweet-sour, canned (Greenwood's) 76
cabbage, red, sweet-sour, in jars (Lord Mott's) 60
carrots:
  diced, canned (Comstock) 19
  sliced, canned (Comstock) 18
  sliced, in jars (Lord Mott's) 24
  sliced, in butter sauce, frozen (Birds Eye) 70
  w/brown sugar glaze, frozen (Birds Eye) 114
cauliflower, frozen (Birds Eye) 21
collard greens, chopped, frozen (Birds Eye) 44
corn:
  on the cob, frozen (Birds Eye), 1 ear* 98
  cut, frozen (Birds Eye) 77
  cut, frozen (Seabrook Farms) 75

in butter sauce, frozen (Birds Eye) 101
cream style, frozen (Birds Eye) 85
and peas, w/tomatoes, frozen (Birds Eye) 71
and carrots and pearl onions, in cream sauce, frozen (Birds Eye) 120
eggplant, sticks, frozen (Mrs. Paul's), 7-oz. pkg. 516
kale, chopped, frozen (Birds Eye) 29
mushrooms:
whole, frozen (Birds Eye) 25
button, canned (Brandywine) 15
button, sliced, canned (Brandywine) 15
cocktail, see "Appetizers & Hors D'Oeuvres," page 146
stems and pieces, canned (Brandywine) 15
w/butter, canned (B in B) 31
mustard greens, chopped, frozen (Birds Eye) 19
okra, whole, frozen (Birds Eye) 27
okra, cut, frozen (Birds Eye) 36
onions:
boiled, canned (O & C) 35
boiled, canned (York County Dutch) 55
boiled, in jars (Lord Mott's) 30
cocktail, see "Relishes," page 38
in cream sauce, frozen (Birds Eye) 122
in cream sauce, frozen (Seabrook Farms) 125
in cream-style sauce, in jars (Lord Mott's) 64
rings, French fried, canned (O & C), 3½-oz. can 618
rings, French fried, frozen (Birds Eye), 4-oz. 336
rings, French fried, frozen (Mrs. Paul's), 5-oz. pkg. 315
peas and carrots, see "peas, green," below
peas, blackeye, frozen (Birds Eye) 122
peas, blackeye, in jars (Lord Mott's) 87
peas, green:
frozen (Birds Eye) 70
in jars (Lord Mott's) 83
w/mushrooms, frozen (Birds Eye) 66
in butter sauce, frozen (Birds Eye) 97
in butter sauce, frozen (Seabrook Farms) 100
in cream sauce, frozen (Birds Eye) 129
in onion sauce, frozen (Seabrook Farms) 96
and carrots, frozen (Birds Eye) 52
and carrots, in jars (Lord Mott's) 54
and celery, frozen (Birds Eye) 58

peas, green, continued

and pearl onions, frozen (Birds Eye) 68
and potatoes, in cream sauce, frozen (Birds Eye) 133

potatoes:

whole, boiled, in jars (Lord Mott's) 59
French fried, frozen (Birds Eye), 17 pieces* 145
French fried, frozen (Seabrook Farms), 17 pieces* 153
French fried, bites, frozen (Birds Eye Tiny Taters), ⅙ pkg. 109
French fried, crinkle cut, frozen (Birds Eye), 17 pieces* 145
French fried, puffs, frozen (Birds Eye), ⅓ pkg. 149
mashed, mix, prepared† (French's) 136
patties, frozen (Birds Eye), 1 patty* 180
whipped, mix, prepared† (Borden's) 83
w/ham, canned (Morton House) 220

potatoes, sweet, in jars (Lord Mott's) 117
potatoes, sweet, candied, frozen (Bird's Eye), 12-oz. pkg. 612
potatoes, sweet, candied, frozen (Mrs. Paul's), 12-oz. pkg. 557
pumpkin, canned (Stokely-Van Camp) 38

spinach:

leaf, frozen (Birds Eye) 24
leaf, frozen (Seabrook Farms) 25
leaf, in jars (Lord Mott's) 22
chopped, frozen (Birds Eye) 23
chopped, in jars (Lord Mott's) 22
chopped, in butter sauce, frozen (Birds Eye) 55
chopped, creamed, frozen (Seabrook Farms) 104
chopped, in cream-style sauce, in jars (Lord Mott's) 48

squash, cooked, frozen (Birds Eye) 43
squash, cooked, frozen (Seabrook Farms) 45
squash, summer, frozen (Birds Eye) 20
succotash, frozen (Birds Eye) 90
tomato paste, see "Tomato Paste & Purée," page 37
tomato purée, see "Tomato Paste & Purée," page 37

tomatoes:

whole, in jars (Lord Mott's) 25
whole, round, peeled, canned (Contadina) 17
baby, sliced, canned (Contadina) 24
stewed, canned (Hunt's) 37
stewed, in jars (Lord Mott's) 25

turnip greens, chopped, frozen (Birds Eye) 22
vegetables, mixed, frozen (Birds Eye) 51
vegetables, mixed, frozen (Seabrook Farms) 50
vegetables, mixed, Chinese, canned (Chun King) 10

vegetables, mixed, Chinese, canned (La Choy)	11
vegetables, mixed, in butter sauce, frozen (Birds Eye)	83
vegetables, mixed, in onion sauce, frozen (Birds Eye)	117
yams, see "potatoes, sweet," page 36	

** As packaged*
*** Approximately ⅓ to ½ cup*
† According to package directions

BEANS, BAKED, ½ cup

See also "Beans, Baked-Style" and page 133

	CALORIES
in New England style sauce (B & M)	180
pea beans, in New England Style sauce (B & M)	180
in tomato sauce (Morton House)	160
w/pork, in tomato sauce (Howard Johnson's)	162

BEANS, BAKED-STYLE, ½ cup

See also "Beans, Baked" and page 133

	CALORIES
in barbecue sauce (Campbell's Barbecue)	171
in molasses sauce (Heinz)	142
in tomato sauce (Heinz)	135
smoke flavored, in tomato sauce (Heinz Campside)	180
w/frankfurters, in tomato sauce (Campbell's)	181
w/frankfurters, in tomato sauce (Heinz Minute Meal)	184
w/ground beef, in barbecue sauce (Campbell's)	148
w/pork, in molasses sauce (Heinz)	152
w/pork, in tomato sauce (Campbell's)	147
w/pork, in tomato sauce (Heinz)	150

TOMATO PASTE & PURÉE

	CALORIES
paste, canned (Contadina), 6-oz. can	182
paste, canned (Hunt's), ½ cup	108
purée, canned (Contadina), ½ cup	46
purée, canned (Hunt's), ½ cup	46
purée, in jars (Lord Mott's), 4 oz.	44

VEGETABLE JUICES, 6-ounce glass

See also page 129

	CALORIES
tomato, bottled (Welch's)	37
tomato, canned (Campbell's)	33
tomato, canned (Heinz)	39
tomato, canned (Hunt's)	38
tomato cocktail, canned (College Inn)	43
vegetable, canned (V-8)	31
vegetable, canned (Vegemato)	32

RELISHES

	CALORIES
carrots, dill (Cresca Cocktail Sticks), 1 carrot*	trace
cauliflower, sweet (Heinz), 1 bud*	9
eggplant, cocktail (Cresca), 1 piece*	trace
olives:	
green, Manzanilla, stuffed (Durkee), 1 olive*	4
green, Manzanilla, stuffed (Grandee), 1 olive*	4
green, Spanish (Vita), 1 olive*	7
green, stuffed, Spanish (Vita), 1 olive*	11
green, queen, stuffed (Durkee), 1 olive*	14
green, queen, stuffed (Grandee), 1 olive*	14
ripe (Vita), 1 olive*	7
ripe, pitted (Durkee), 1 olive*	7
ripe, pitted (Grandee), 1 olive*	7
ripe, pitted (Lindsay), 1 olive*	6
onions:	
sour, cocktail (Cresca), 1 onion*	trace
sour, cocktail (Crosse & Blackwell), 1 onion*	trace
sour, cocktail (Heinz), 1 onion*	trace
spiced (Heinz), 1 onion*	5
peppers, hot chili (Cresca), 1 pepper*	trace
pickle relish:	
barbecue (Crosse & Blackwell), 1 tbsp.	22
barbecue (Heinz), 1 tbsp.	32
corn (Crosse & Blackwell), 1 tbsp.	15

hamburger (Crosse & Blackwell), 1 tbsp. 20
hamburger (Heinz), 1 tbsp. 17
hot dog (Crosse & Blackwell), 1 tbsp. 22
hot dog (Heinz), 1 tbsp. 22
hot pepper (Crosse & Blackwell), 1 tbsp. 22
India (Crosse & Blackwell), 1 tbsp. 26
India (Heinz), 1 tbsp. 28
piccalilli (Crosse & Blackwell), 1 tbsp. 26
piccalilli (Heinz), 1 tbsp. 19
sweet (Crosse & Blackwell), 1 tbsp. 26
sweet (Heinz), 1 tbsp. 20

pickles, dill and sour:
whole (Bond's Flavor-Pack Dills), 1 pickle* 1
whole (Bond's Fresh-Pack Dills), 1 pickle* 2
whole (Bond's Fresh-Pack Kosher Dills), 1 pickle* 2
whole (Heinz Fresh Kosher Dills), 1 pickle* 4
whole (Heinz Fresh Kosher Baby Dills), 1 pickle* 2
whole (Heinz Genuine Dills), 1 pickle* 12
whole (Heinz Processed Dills), 1 pickle* 2
whole (Heinz Sour Gherkins), 1 pickle* 9
whole (L & S Dills), 1 pickle* 1
whole (L & S Fresh-Pack Kosher Dills), 1 pickle* 2
spears (Bond's Fresh-Pack Dill Spears), 1 piece* 2
spears (Bond's Fresh-Pack Kosher Dill Spears), 1 piece* 2
slices (Crosse & Blackwell Kosher Dill Slices), 1 tbsp. 2
slices (Heinz Hamburger Dill Slices), 3 pieces* 1

pickles, sweet:
whole (Bond's Sweet Gherkins), 1 pickle* 19
whole (Heinz Midget Gherkins), 1 pickle* 5
whole (Heinz Sweet Gherkins), 1 pickle* 25
whole (Heinz Sweet Pickles), 1 pickle* 45
whole (L & S Sweet Pickles), 1 pickle* 19
spears (Crosse & Blackwell Fresh Cucumber Spears), 1 piece* 28
spears (Heinz Sweet Pickle Spears), 1 piece* 18
sticks (Heinz Sweet Pickle Sticks), 1 piece* 13
strips (Heinz Candied Dill Strips), 1 piece* 35
slices (Bond's Fresh-Pack Cucumber Slices), 3 pieces* 23
slices (Crosse & Blackwell Fresh Cucumber Slices), 1 tbsp. 15
slices (Crosse & Blackwell Sweet Chips), 1 tbsp. 17
slices (Heinz Candied Krink-L-Chips), 3 pieces* 33
slices (Heinz Fresh Cucumber Slices), 3 pieces* 15

pickles, sweet, continued

slices (Heinz Sweet Cucumber Disks), 3 pieces* 15
slices (Heinz Sweet Pickle Chips), 3 pieces* 15
w/mustard (Crosse & Blackwell Chow Chow), 1 tbsp. 6
w/mustard (Heinz Sweet Mustard Pickles), 1 tbsp. 30
watermelon rind (Crosse & Blackwell), 1 tbsp. 38

* *As packaged*

MEAT, POULTRY, FISH AND SEAFOOD

8

MEAT ENTREES

See also "Bacon, Luncheon Meat & Sausage," "Frozen Dinners," etc. and pages 136-143

	CALORIES
beef:	
sliced, in barbecue sauce, frozen (Banquet), 5-oz. pkg.	174
sliced, in barbecue sauce, frozen (Banquet Buffet Supper), 8 oz.	294
sliced, in gravy, frozen (Banquet), 5-oz. pkg.	158
sliced, in gravy, frozen (Banquet Buffet Supper), 8 oz.	238
in red wine sauce, frozen (Seabrook Farms), 6-oz. pkg.	265
chop suey, see "Chinese Foods," pages 52-53	
goulash, canned (Heinz Minute Meal), 8½-oz. can	253
goulash, w/noodles, frozen (Seabrook Farms), 7-oz. pkg.	198
goulash, w/noodles, packaged, prepared* (Chef Boy-Ar-Dee Dinner), 1 cup	351
w/macaroni, canned, see "Macaroni: Canned, Frozen & Mixes," page 56	
w/noodles, see "Noodles: Canned & Mixes," page 57	
pot pie, frozen (Banquet), 8-oz. pie	412
pot pie, frozen (Swanson), 8-oz. pie	443
Stroganoff, packaged, prepared* (Chef Boy-Ar-Dee Dinner), 1 cup	371
Stroganoff, packaged, prepared* (Lipton Main Dish), 1 cup	304
Stroganoff, packaged, prepared* (Noodle-Roni), 1 cup	340
chili con carne, see "Mexican Foods," pages 53-54	
frankfurters:	
all beef (Oscar Mayer), 1.6-oz. frank	139
all beef (Oscar Mayer Machiaeh), 2-oz. frank	174
all beef (Vienna), 1.6-oz. frank	130
all meat (Oscar Mayer), 1.6-oz. frank	140
and beans, canned, see "Beans, Baked-Style," page 37	
and beans, frozen dinner, see "Frozen Dinners," page 52	

ham:
cured, cooked, see "Bacon, Luncheon Meat & Sausage," page 48
cured, smoked, aged (Amber Brand Smithfield), 4 oz. 440
cured, smoked, cooked (Oscar Mayer Jubilee, Boneless), 4 oz. 252
cured, smoke flavored, canned (Oscar Mayer Boneless), 4 oz. 160
cured, smoke flavored, canned (Swift Boneless), 4 oz. 189
in barbecue sauce, frozen (Banquet), 4½-oz. pkg. 184
hash, corned beef, canned:
(Armour Star), 1 cup 435
(Bounty), 1 cup 405
(Broadcast), 1 cup 484
(Hormel Mary Kitchen), 8 oz.** 304
(Morton House), 1 cup 488
(Wilson's Certified), 1 cup 459
hash, roast beef, canned (Hormel Mary Kitchen), 8 oz.** 376
meatballs, in gravy, canned (Chef Boy-Ar-Dee), 1 cup 315
pork and beans, see "Beans, Baked-Style," page 37
pork chops, fresh, pan-broiled (Wilson's Big Eye), 4 oz. 344
Salisbury steak, in gravy, canned (Morton House), 12¾-oz. can 835
Sloppy Joe, canned (Gebhardt), 8 oz. 280
Sloppy Joe, canned (Morton House), 1 cup 471
Sloppy Joe, frozen (Banquet), 5-oz. pkg. 250
stew, beef:
canned (Armour Star), 1 cup 200
canned (B & M), 1 cup 163
canned (Bounty), 1 cup 213
canned (Dinty Moore), 1 cup 198
canned (Heinz Minute Meal), 1 cup 253
canned (Morton House), 1 cup 312
canned (James River Smithfield), 1 cup 186
canned (Wilson's Certified), 1 cup 202
frozen (Lambrecht), 16-oz. pkg. 432
frozen (Seabrook Farms), 8-oz. pkg. 229
stew, lamb, canned (B & M), 1 cup 247
stew, meatball, canned (Chef Boy-Ar-Dee), 1 cup 218

* *According to package directions*
** *Approximately ¾ cup to 1 cup*

POULTRY ENTREES

See also "Frozen Dinners" and pages 136-141

	CALORIES
chicken:	
boned, w/broth, canned (Banquet), 5-oz. can	278
boned, w/broth, canned (College Inn), 5-oz. can	374
boned, solid pack, canned (Richardson & Robbins), 5½-oz. can	328
whole, fried, frozen (Banquet), 1 pkg.	1442
à la king, canned (College Inn), 1 cup	266
à la king, canned (Richardson & Robbins), 1 cup	332
à la king, frozen (Banquet), 5-oz. pkg.	141
à la king, frozen (Lambrecht), 15-oz. pkg.	585
cacciatore, breast of, frozen (Seabrook Farms), 7-oz. pkg.	248
chop suey, see "Frozen Entrees," page 138	
chow mein, see "Chinese Foods," page 53	
croquettes, w/fricassee sauce, frozen (Howard Johnson's), 12-oz. pkg.	536
dinner, packaged, prepared* (Lipton Chicken Baronet), 1 cup	256
dinner, packaged, prepared* (Lipton Chicken La Scala), 1 cup	262
and dumplings, canned (Morton House), 1 cup	363
fricassee, canned (College Inn), 1 cup	240
fricassee, canned (Richardson & Robbins), 1 cup	229
and noodle casserole, frozen (Howard Johnson's), 12-oz. pkg.	384
and noodle dinner, canned (Heinz Minute Meal), 8½-oz. can**	186
w/noodles, see "Noodles: Canned & Mixes," page 57	
pot pie, frozen (Banquet), 8-oz. pie	412
pot pie, frozen (Morton), 8-oz. pie	460
pot pie, frozen (Swanson), 8-oz. pie	503
and rice, w/vegetables, canned (Morton House), 1 cup	460
smoked, pressed, see "Bacon, Luncheon Meat & Sausage," page 48	
stew, canned (B & M), 1 cup	168
stew, canned (Bounty), 1 cup	221
stew, Brunswick, canned (James River Smithfield), 1 cup	206
stew, w/dumplings, canned (Heinz Minute Meal), 8½-oz. can**	202
turkey:	
w/giblet gravy, frozen (Banquet), 5-oz. pkg.	128
w/giblet gravy, frozen (Banquet Buffet Supper), 8 oz.	170
dinner, packaged, prepared* (Lipton Turkey Primavera), 1 cup	314
pot pie, frozen (Banquet), 8-oz. pie	400
pot pie, frozen (Morton), 8-oz. pie	400

turkey, continued

pot pie, frozen (Swanson), 8-oz. pie 442
pot pie, frozen (Swanson), 16-oz. pie 608

* *According to package directions*
** *Approximately ¾ cup to 1 cup*

FISH & SEAFOOD

See also "Frozen Dinners" and pages 136, 138-141

CALORIES

anchovy paste, see "Meat, Fish & Poultry Spreads," page 50
catfish, ocean, fillets, uncooked, frozen (Gorton's), 16-oz. pkg. 286
clam chowder, see "Soups, Broths & Chowders," page 30
clam cocktail, in jars (Sau-Sea), 4-oz jar 99
clam croquettes, w/clam sauce, frozen (Howard Johnson's), 12-oz. pkg. 608
clam sticks, precooked, frozen (Mrs. Paul's), 8-oz. pkg. 458
clams:

whole, canned, meat only (Doxsee), ½ cup 97
whole, canned, half meat/half liquid (Doxsee), 1 cup 116
chopped, canned, meat only (Doxsee), ½ cup 98
chopped, canned, half meat/half liquid (Doxsee), 1 cup 118
chopped, canned, half meat/half liquid (Snow's), 1 cup 128
minced, canned, meat only (Doxsee), ½ cup 98
minced, canned, half meat/half liquid (Doxsee), 1 cup 118
minced, canned, half meat/half liquid (Snow's), 1 cup 128
fried, frozen (Howard Johnson's), 7-oz. pkg. 357
fried, frozen (Lord Mott's), 7-oz. pkg. 450
soft shell, fried, frozen (Lord Mott's), 7-oz. pkg. 438
steamed, in shells, canned (Doxsee), 6 clams* 26
steamed, in shells, canned (Lord Mott's), 6 clams* 35

cod:

fillets, uncooked, frozen (Gorton's), 16-oz. pkg. 355
fillets, uncooked, frozen (San Juan), 16-oz. pkg. 336
fillets, uncooked, frozen (Ship Ahoy), 16-oz. pkg. 336
breaded, frozen (Gorton's), 11-oz. pkg. 331
sticks, precooked, frozen (Birds Eye), 8-oz. pkg. 552
sticks, precooked, frozen (Gorton's), 16-oz. pkg. 830

crab:

canned (Bumble Bee), 7½-oz. can 221
canned (Icy Point), 7½-oz. can 221
canned (Pillar Rock), 7½-oz. can 221

frozen (San Juan), 8-oz. pkg. 220
frozen (Ship Ahoy), 8-oz. pkg. 220
cocktail, in jars (Sau-Sea), 4-oz. jar 107
à la king, frozen (Lambrecht), 11-oz. pkg. 319
cakes, precooked, frozen (Lord Mott's), 6-oz. pkg. 491
deviled, frozen (Lord Mott's), 10-oz. pkg. 523
deviled, frozen (Mrs. Paul's), 6-oz. pkg. 345
sticks, precooked, frozen (Lord Mott's), 8-oz. pkg. 484
eel, smoked (Vita), 4 oz. 185
fish balls, precooked, frozen (Gorton's), 7-oz. pkg. 395
fish bites, precooked, frozen (Birds Eye), 8-oz. pkg. 552
fish cakes, precooked, frozen (Gorton's), 8-oz. pkg. 463
fish cakes, precooked, frozen (Mrs. Paul's), 8-oz. pkg. 422
fish flakes, canned (Gorton's), 7-oz. can 145
fish roe, canned (Gorton's), 8-oz. can 136
fish sticks, precooked, frozen (Mrs. Paul's), 9-oz. pkg. 495
flounder:
fillets, uncooked, frozen (Gorton's), 16-oz. pkg. 313
fillets, uncooked, frozen (San Juan), 16-oz. pkg. 308
fillets, uncooked, frozen (Ship Ahoy), 16-oz. pkg. 308
precooked, frozen (Gorton's), 9½-oz. pkg. 517
stuffed, precooked, frozen (Lord Mott's), 10-oz. pkg. 720
gefilte fish, 1 piece:
canned (Manischewitz—2-piece/15½-oz. can) 100
canned (Mother's—2-piece/15½-oz. can) 112
canned (Mother's—5-piece/27-oz. can) 90
canned (Rokeach—4-piece/14-oz. can) 28
canned (Rokeach Old Vienna—4-piece/14-oz. can) 37
canned (Rokeach—6-piece/38-oz. can) 54
in jars (Manischewitz Jumbo—8-piece/2-lb. jar) 64
in jars (Mother's—4-piece/10-oz. jar) 52
in jars (Mother's—4-piece/1-lb. jar) 58
in jars (Mother's—6-piece/1-lb. jar) 49
in jars (Mother's—8-piece/2-lb. jar) 78
in jars (Mother's—12-piece/2-lb. jar) 49
saltfree, in jars (Mother's—6-piece/15-oz. jar) 46
whitefish-pike, in jars (Manischewitz—2-piece/15½-oz. jar) 81
haddock, fillets, uncooked, frozen (Gorton's), 16-oz. pkg. 360
haddock, au gratin, frozen (Howard Johnson's), 12-oz. pkg. 396
halibut, fillets, uncooked, frozen (San Juan), 12-oz. pkg. 429
halibut, fillets, uncooked, frozen (Ship Ahoy), 12-oz. pkg. 429
herring, in sour cream, in jars (Vita), 8-oz. jar 392

herring, pickled, in jars (Vita Bismarck), 5-oz. jar 270
oysters, frozen (San Juan), 10-oz. pkg. 238
oysters, frozen (Ship Ahoy), 10-oz. pkg. 238
perch, ocean, fillets, frozen (Gorton's), 16-oz. pkg. 400
salmon:
  blueback, canned (Icy Point), 7¾-oz. can 395
  chinook, canned (Bumble Bee), 7¾-oz. can 467
  chum, canned (Bumble Bee), 7¾-oz. can 270
  coho, canned (Bumble Bee), 7¾-oz. can 355
  pink, canned (Bumble Bee), 7¾-oz. can 320
  pink, canned (Icy Point), 7¼-oz. can 308
  pink, canned (Pink Beauty), 7¼-oz. can 308
  red, canned (Bumble Bee), 7¾-oz. can 391
  red, canned (Pillar Rock), 7¾-oz. can 395
  smoked (Vita), 4 oz. 280
salt fish, canned (Gorton's), 11-oz. can 274
sardines:
  in oil, canned (Crown), 3¾-oz. can** 192
  in oil, canned (King Oscar), 3¾-oz. can** 172
  in oil, canned (Underwood), 3¾-oz. can** 167
  in mustard sauce, canned (Underwood), 3¾-oz. can 158
  in tomato sauce, canned (Eatwell), 15-oz. can 838
  in tomato sauce, canned (Underwood), 3¾-oz. can 141
  smoked, canned (Snow's Norwegian style), 3¾-oz. can** 175
scallops, uncooked, frozen (Gorton's), 12-oz. pkg. 252
scallops, precooked, frozen (Birds Eye), 7-oz. pkg. 420
scallops, precooked, frozen (Gorton's), 7-oz. pkg. 304
scallops, precooked, frozen (Mrs. Paul's), 7-oz. pkg. 301
seafood croquettes, w/Newburg sauce, frozen
  (Howard Johnson's), 12-oz. pkg. 564
shad roe, canned (Bumble Bee), 7¾-oz. can 259
shrimp:
  canned, drained (Bumble Bee), 4½ oz. 151
  w/cocktail sauce, in jars (Sau-Sea), 4-oz. jar 112
  w/cocktail sauce, in jars (Sau-Sea), 6-oz. jar 121
  breaded, fried, frozen (Mrs. Paul's), 6-oz. pkg. 388
  breaded, fried, frozen (Chicken of the Sea), 8-oz. pkg. 512
  croquettes, w/Newburg sauce, frozen (Howard Johnson's), 12-oz. pkg. 476
sole, fillets, uncooked (Ship Ahoy), 16-oz pkg. 309
sturgeon, smoked (Vita), 4 oz. 280

tuna:
- light, in oil, canned, chunk-pack (Bumble Bee), 6½-oz. can** 304
- light, in oil, canned, chunk-pack (Chicken of the Sea), 6½-oz. can** 384
- light, in oil, canned, chunk-pack (Icy Point), 6½-oz. can** 279
- light, in oil, canned, chunk-pack (Snow Mist), 6½-oz. can** 279
- light, in oil, canned, chunk-pack (Star-Kist), 6½-oz. can** 289
- white, in oil, canned, chunk-pack (Bumble Bee), 6½-oz. can** 304
- white, in oil, canned, chunk-pack (Chicken of the Sea), 6½-oz. can**..324
- white, in oil, canned, chunk-pack (Star-Kist), 6½-oz. can** 289
- white, in oil, canned, solid-pack (Bumble Bee), 7-oz. can** 318
- white, in oil, canned, solid-pack (Chicken of the Sea), 7-oz. can** ...328
- white, in oil, canned, solid-pack (Pillar Rock), 7-oz. can** 290
- white, in oil, canned, solid-pack (Star-Kist), 7-oz. can** 304
- white, in water, canned, solid-pack (Chicken of the Sea), 7-oz. can** ..216
- white, in water, canned, solid-pack (Star Kist), 7-oz. can** 210
- pot pie, frozen (Banquet), 8-oz. pie 478
- pot pie, frozen (Star-Kist), 8-oz. pie 397
- pot pie, frozen (Morton), 8-oz. pie 385
- and noodle casserole, frozen (Howard Johnson's), 12-oz. pkg. 576

whitefish, smoked (Vita), 4 oz. 400
whiting, fillets, uncooked, frozen (Gorton's), 16-oz. pkg. 354

* *As packaged*
** *Drained of oil or water*

BACON, LUNCHEON MEAT & SAUSAGE

See also "Meat, Fish & Poultry Spreads" and pages 142-144

CALORIES

bacon, beef (Vienna), 1 slice*, cooked 36
bacon, pork:
- regular sliced (Oscar Mayer Sugar Cured), 1 slice*, cooked 59
- thick sliced (Oscar Mayer Ranch Style), 1 slice*, cooked 97
- thin sliced (Festival—1-lb. pkg.), 1 slice*, cooked 34
- thin sliced (Festival—2-lb. pkg.), 1 slice*, cooked 46
- thin sliced (Morrell), 1 slice*, cooked 37
- thin sliced (Oscar Mayer Wafer Thin), 1 slice*, cooked 35
- prefried, canned (Oscar Mayer), 1 slice* 63
- Canadian style (Festival), 1 slice*, cooked 32
- Canadian style (Oscar Mayer—6-oz. pkg.), 1 slice*, cooked 55

bacon, continued

Canadian style (Oscar Mayer—5-oz. pkg.), 1 slice*, cooked 42
barbecue loaf (Oscar Mayer Bar-B-Que), 8-oz. pkg. 368
barbecue loaf (Oscar Mayer Bar-B-Que), 1 slice* 44
beef, chopped, canned (Armour Star), 12-oz. can 1190
beef, chopped, canned (Wilson's Certified Bif), 12-oz. can 1090
beef, corned (Vienna), 4-oz. pkg. 286
beef, corned, chopped, canned (Wilson's Certified), 12-oz. can 720
beef, corned, chopped, pressed (Buddig), 3-oz. pkg. 98
beef, corned, jellied loaf (Oscar Mayer), 8-oz. pkg. 312
beef, corned, jellied loaf (Oscar Mayer), 1 slice* 34
beef, dried, in jars (Armour Star), 5-oz. jar 234
beef, jellied loaf (Oscar Mayer), 8-oz. pkg. 328
beef, jellied loaf (Oscar Mayer), 1 slice* 38
beef, smoked, chopped, pressed (Buddig), 3-oz. pkg. 103
bologna:

pure beef (Oscar Mayer), 8-oz. pkg. 728
pure beef (Oscar Mayer), 1 slice* 69
pure beef (Oscar Mayer Lebanon), 8-oz. pkg. 496
pure beef (Oscar Mayer Lebanon), 1 slice* 47
pure beef (Vienna), 4-oz. pkg. 298
all meat (Oscar Mayer), 8-oz. pkg. 704
all meat (Oscar Mayer), 1 slice* 66

braunschweiger (Oscar Mayer), 9-oz. pkg. 963
cervelat, see "thuringer cervelat," page 50
chicken, smoked, chopped, pressed (Buddig), 3-oz. pkg. 109
cocktail loaf (Oscar Mayer), 8-oz. pkg. 504
cocktail loaf (Oscar Mayer), 1 slice* 60
corned beef, see "beef, corned," above
ham, cooked (Danola Danish), 4-oz. pkg. 116
ham, cooked, smoked (Oscar Mayer), 5-oz. pkg. 215
ham, cooked, smoked (Oscar Mayer), 1 slice* 43
ham, chopped (Oscar Mayer), 8-oz. pkg. 504
ham, chopped (Oscar Mayer), 1 slice* 60
ham, chopped, canned (Armour Star), 12-oz. can 1004
ham, minced (Oscar Mayer), 8-oz. pkg. 544
ham, minced (Oscar Mayer), 1 slice* 64
ham, smoked, chopped, pressed (Buddig), 3-oz. pkg. 106
ham and cheese loaf (Oscar Mayer), 8-oz. pkg. 560
ham and cheese loaf (Oscar Mayer), 1 slice* 66
head cheese (Oscar Mayer), 8-oz. pkg. 384
head cheese (Oscar Mayer), 1 slice* 50
honey seasoned loaf (Oscar Mayer), 8-oz. pkg. 352

liver cheese (Oscar Mayer), 8-oz. pkg. 608
liver cheese (Oscar Mayer), 1 slice* 101
luncheon meat, canned:
  (Broadcast), 12-oz. can 1111
  (Spam), 12-oz. can 1176
  (Treet), 12-oz. can 1014
  (Wilson's Certified Mor), 12-oz. can 1063
luncheon meat, all meat loaf (Oscar Mayer), 8-oz. pkg. 752
luncheon meat, all meat loaf (Oscar Mayer), 1 slice* 89
luxury loaf (Oscar Mayer), 8-oz. pkg. 312
luxury loaf (Oscar Mayer), 1 slice* 37
minced roll sausage (Oscar Mayer), 8-oz. pkg. 512
minced roll sausage (Oscar Mayer), 1 slice* 49
New England Brand sausage (Oscar Mayer), 8-oz. pkg. 352
New England Brand sausage (Oscar Mayer), 1 slice* 33
old fashioned loaf (Oscar Mayer), 8-oz. pkg. 440
old fashioned loaf (Oscar Mayer), 1 slice* 52
olive loaf (Oscar Mayer), 8-oz. pkg. 320
olive loaf (Oscar Mayer), 1 slice* 38
pastrami, pure beef (Vienna), 4-oz. pkg. 272
pastrami, all beef, smoked, chopped, pressed (Buddig), 3-oz. pkg. 98
peppered loaf (Oscar Mayer), 8-oz. pkg. 336
peppered loaf (Oscar Mayer), 1 slice* 40
pickle and pimiento loaf (Oscar Mayer), 8-oz. pkg. 504
pickle and pimiento loaf (Oscar Mayer), 1 slice* 60
picnic loaf (Oscar Mayer), 8-oz. pkg. 464
picnic loaf (Oscar Mayer), 1 slice* 55
pork sausage (Oscar Mayer Little Friers), 1-lb. pkg., cooked 816
pork sausage (Oscar Mayer Little Friers), 1 link*, cooked 51
salami:
  pure beef (Oscar Mayer Pure Beef Cotto), 8-oz. pkg. 416
  pure beef (Oscar Mayer Pure Beef Cotto), 1 slice* 40
  pure beef (Vienna), 4-oz. pkg. 300
  all meat (Oscar Mayer All Meat Cotto), 8-oz. pkg. 520
  all meat (Oscar Mayer All Meat Cotto), 1 slice* 50
  all meat (Oscar Mayer Hard Salami), 8-oz. pkg. 904
  all meat (Oscar Mayer Hard Salami), 1 slice* 38
  all meat (Oscar Mayer Salami for Beer), 8-oz. pkg. 512
  all meat (Oscar Mayer Salami for Beer), 1 slice* 49
scrapple (Oscar Mayer), 1-lb. can 704
smokie link sausage:
  (Oscar Mayer), 12-oz. pkg. 1008
  (Oscar Mayer), 1 link* 126

smokie link sausage, continued
w/cheese (Oscar Mayer Smokies), 12-oz. pkg. 996
w/cheese (Oscar Mayer Smokies), 1 link* 125
summer sausage, pure beef (Oscar Mayer), 8-oz. pkg. 659
summer sausage, pure beef (Oscar Mayer), 1 slice* 62
thuringer cervelat (Oscar Mayer), 8-oz. pkg. 720
thuringer cervelat (Oscar Mayer), 1 slice* 68
turkey breast (Oscar Mayer), 5-oz. pkg. 150
turkey breast (Oscar Mayer), 1 slice* 25
turkey, smoked, chopped, pressed (Buddig), 3-oz. pkg. 108
Vienna sausage, see "Appetizers and Hors D'Oeuvres," page 147

* *As packaged*

MEAT, FISH & POULTRY SPREADS, 1 tablespoon

See also page 143

CALORIES

anchovy paste (Crosse & Blackwell) 20
chicken (Underwood) 31
chili meat (Gebhardt) 37
ham, deviled (Armour Star) 40
ham, deviled (Underwood) 45
ham, deviled, Smithfield (Amber Brand Smithfield) 47
liver, pâté (Sell's) 43
liverwurst (Underwood) 43
meat, potted (Armour Star) 31

PIZZA, FROZEN DINNERS, CHINESE AND MEXICAN FOODS 9

PIZZA, 1 whole pie*, as packaged

See also page 145

	CALORIES
cheese:	
frozen (Buitoni Instant), 2¾ oz.	139
frozen (Chef Boy-Ar-Dee), 12½ oz.	798
frozen (Chef Boy-Ar-Dee Little), 2½ oz.	164
frozen (Lambrecht), 13 oz.	910
frozen (Roman), 2¾ oz.	175
mix, prepared** (Chef Boy-Ar-Dee), 15.6 oz.	912
pepperoni, frozen (Chef Boy-Ar-Dee), 14 oz.	906
pepperoni, frozen (Roman), 3¼ oz.	253
pepperoni, mix, prepared** (Chef Boy-Ar-Dee), 16.8 oz.	1050
sausage:	
frozen (Chef Boy-Ar-Dee), 13.2 oz.	876
frozen (Chef Boy-Ar-Dee Little), 2½ oz.	169
frozen (Lambrecht), 14 oz.	1008
frozen (Roman), 3¼	234
mix, prepared** (Chef Boy-Ar-Dee), 16.8 oz.	1014

* *Note variations in size*
** *According to package directions*

FROZEN DINNERS, 1 complete dinner*, as packaged

See also pages 136 and 138

	CALORIES
beans and franks (Banquet), 10¾ oz.	687
beans and franks (Morton), 12 oz.	553

frozen dinners, continued

beef (Banquet), 11 oz. 295
beef (Morton), 11 oz. 316
beef, chopped (Banquet), 9 oz. 386
chicken, fried (Banquet), 11 oz. 542
chicken, fried (Morton), 11 oz. 436
enchilada, beef (Banquet), 12½ oz. 467
enchilada, cheese (Banquet), 12½ oz. 482
fish (Morton), 8 oz. 221
haddock (Banquet), 8.8 oz. 424
ham (Banquet), 10 oz. 352
ham (Morton), 10 oz. 443
Italian (Banquet), 11 oz. 414
macaroni and beef (Morton), 11 oz. 327
macaroni and cheese (Banquet), 12 oz. 342
macaroni and cheese (Morton), 12 oz. 393
meat loaf (Banquet), 11 oz. 420
meat loaf (Morton), 11 oz. 389
Mexican (Banquet), 16¼ oz. 569
Salisbury steak (Banquet), 11 oz. 335
Salisbury steak (Morton), 11 oz. 348
shrimp (Morton), 7 oz. 231
spaghetti and meatballs (Banquet), 11½ oz. 423
spaghetti and meatballs (Morton), 11 oz. 364
tuna (Star-Kist), 7 oz. 204
turkey (Banquet), 11½ oz. 280
turkey (Morton), 12 oz. 460

* *Note variations in size*

CHINESE FOODS, 1 cup, except as noted

See also "Frozen Dinners" and pages 136 and 138

CALORIES

Chinese vegetables, see "Vegetables," page 33
chop suey, frozen, see "Frozen Entrees," page 138
chow mein, canned, without noodles:
  beef (Chun King) 150
  beef (Chun King—divider-pak) 59
  beef (La Choy) 77
  beef (La Choy—bi-pack) 90
  chicken (Chun King) 100

chicken (Chun King—divider-pak) 107
chicken (La Choy) 74
chicken (La Choy—bi-pack) 118
meatless (Chun King) 83
meatless (La Choy) 49
mushroom (Chun King—divider-pak) 50
mushroom (La Choy—bi-pack) 81
pork (Chun King—divider-pak) 170
shrimp (Chun King—divider-pak) 189
shrimp (La Choy) 75
shrimp (La Choy—bi-pack) 110
chow mein, frozen, see "Frozen Entrees," pages 138-139
chow mein noodles, canned (Chun King) 211
chow mein noodles, canned (La Choy) 258
egg foo young, frozen (Chun King), 12-oz. pkg. 240
egg rolls, see "Frozen Snacks & Hors D'Oeuvres," page 145
rice, fried:
chicken, canned (Chun King) 257
chicken, canned (La Choy) 274
w/chicken, frozen (Chun King) 309
w/meat, frozen (Chun King) 317
meatless, canned (Chun King) 186
pork, canned (Chun King) 249
pork, canned (La Choy) 274
shrimp, canned (Chun King) 230
shrimp, frozen (Temple) 297

MEXICAN FOODS

See also "Frozen Dinners" and pages 136-140

CALORIES

beans, pinto, chili, refried, see "Vegetables," page 33
burrito rolls, see "Frozen Snacks & Hors D'Oeuvres," page 145
chili con carne, canned, without beans, 1 cup:
(Armour Star) 438
(Austex) 390
(Gebhardt) 437
(Gebhardt Chunky Beef) 497
(Gebhardt Longhorn) 480
(Old El Paso) 402
(Stokely-Van Camp) 450
(Wilson's Certified) 480

chili con carne, canned, with beans, 1 cup:
- (Armour Star) 358
- (Austex) 353
- (Bounty) 299
- (Broadcast) 401
- (Gebhardt) 443
- (Gebhardt Instant) 478
- (Gebhardt Longhorn) 425
- (Heinz Minute Meal) 352
- (Hormel) 357
- (James River Smithfield) 297
- (Old El Paso) 420
- (Stokely-Van Camp) 334
- (Wilson's Certified) 360

chili con carne, frozen, see "Frozen Entrees," page 138
chili peppers, green, whole, canned (Old El Paso), 4-oz. can 24
chili peppers, green, roasted, peeled, chopped, canned (Old El Paso), 4-oz. can 32
chili peppers, Jalapeno, in jars (Old El Paso), 10-oz. jar 90
enchilada sauce, see "Sauces," page 67
enchiladas, beef, w/gravy, canned (Old El Paso), 1 enchilada* 119
enchiladas, frozen, see "Frozen Entrees," page 139
garbanzos, canned (Old El Paso), ½ cup 103
rice, Mexican, canned (Gebhardt), 4 oz. 208
taco filling, beef, canned (Old El Paso), 7½-oz. can 427
tacos, beef, see "Frozen Entrees," page 140
tacos, beef, cocktail, see "Frozen Snacks & Hors D'Oeuvres," page 146
tamales, canned or in jars, 1 tamale*:
- (Armour Star) 92
- (Austex) 112
- (Gebhardt) 119
- (Old El Paso) 81
- (Wilson's Certified) 100

tamales, frozen, see "Frozen Entrees," page 140
tortillas, canned (Old El Paso), 1 tortilla* 40
tortillas, frozen (Patio—cooking pouch), 1 tortilla* 22

* *As packaged*

PASTA AND RICE 10

PASTA, DRY

As you may know, you can have your pasta (and eat more of it too) by cooking dry forms of macaroni and spaghetti "until tender." Or, to put it another way, the longer you cook these foods, the fewer calories they contain. (This is also true of egg noodles; however, after 8 minutes of cooking, noodles tend to get soggy.) For example, spaghetti cooked 12 minutes has more calories than spaghetti cooked 14 minutes—which, in turn, has more calories than spaghetti cooked 16 or 18 minutes. Bear this in mind as you note the figures below. It is likely that they reflect variations in cooking time as much as—or more than—a difference in the products.

	CALORIES
egg noodles:	
all varieties (Goodman's), cooked*, 1 cup	177
all varieties, except spinach (La Rosa), cooked*, 1 cup	189
all varieties (Pennsylvania Dutch), cooked*, 1 cup	200
all varieties (Prince), cooked*, 1 cup	192
all varieties (Ronzoni), cooked*, 1 cup	200
spinach (La Rosa), cooked*, 1 cup	198
macaroni:	
all varieties (Goodman's), cooked**, 1 cup	150
all varieties (Goodman's), cooked†, 1 cup	185
all varieties (La Rosa), cooked**, 1 cup	170
all varieties (La Rosa), cooked†, 1 cup	190
all varieties (Prince), cooked**, 1 cup	162
all varieties (Prince), cooked†, 1 cup	182
all varieties (Ronzoni), cooked**, 1 cup	155
all varieties (Ronzoni), cooked†, 1 cup	192
spaghetti:	
all varieties (Buitoni), cooked**, 1 cup	163
all varieties (Buitoni), cooked†, 1 cup	204

spaghetti, continued

all varieties (Goodman's), cooked**, 1 cup 150
all varieties (Goodman's), cooked†, 1 cup 185
all varieties (La Rosa), cooked**, 1 cup 161
all varieties (La Rosa), cooked†, 1 cup 174
all varieties (Prince), cooked**, 1 cup 152
all varieties (Prince), cooked†, 1 cup 193
all varieties (Ronzoni), cooked**, 1 cup 155
all varieties (Ronzoni), cooked†, 1 cup 192

** About 8 minutes*
*** 14–20 minutes, until tender*
† 8–10 minutes, until firm (al dente)

MACARONI: CANNED, FROZEN & MIXES

See also "Frozen Dinners," "Pasta, Dry" and pages 136-140

CALORIES

w/beef, in tomato sauce, canned
(Chef Boy-Ar-Dee Beefaroni), 1 cup 237
w/beef, in tomato sauce, canned (Franco-American), 1 cup 241
w/beef, in tomato sauce, canned (Morton House), 1 cup 497
w/beef, in tomato sauce, frozen (Banquet Buffet Supper), 8 oz. 257
and cheese:
frozen (Banquet), 8-oz. pkg.* 280
frozen (Banquet), 20-oz. pkg. 742
frozen (Howard Johnson's), 12-oz. pkg. 660
frozen (Lambrecht), 8-oz.* 232
frozen (Morton), 8-oz. pkg.* 287
mix, prepared** (Golden Grain Stir-N-Serv), 1 cup 366
mix, prepared** (Mac-A-Roni & Cheddar), 1 cup 288
w/cheese sauce, canned (Franco-American), 1 cup 227
w/cheese sauce, canned (Heinz), 1 cup 231
w/cheese sauce, canned (MacaroniO's), 1 cup 182
w/cheese flavored sauce, mix, prepared** (Scallop-A-Roni), 1 cup 276
w/cheese flavored sauce, and peas, mix, prepared**
(Noodle-Roni Casserole), 1 cup 291
w/chili flavored sauce, mix, prepared**
(Fiesta-Mac-A-Roni), 1 cup 269
creole style, canned (Heinz Minute Meal), 8¾-oz. can 169

** Approximately ¾ cup to 1 cup*
*** According to package directions*

NOODLES: CANNED & MIXES, 1 cup, except as noted

See also "Pasta, Dry" and pages 136-141

	CALORIES
w/beef, canned (Heinz Minute Meal), 8½-oz. can*	171
w/beef, in gravy, in jars (College Inn)	237
w/beef, in tomato sauce, in jars (College Inn)	237
and chicken casserole, see "Poultry Entrees," page 43	
and chicken dinner, see "Poultry Entrees," page 43	
w/chicken, in jars (College Inn)	266
w/chicken flavored sauce and almonds, mix, prepared** (Noodle-Roni Chick'n Almonds)	251
w/chicken meat sauce, mix, prepared** (Twist-A-Roni)	249
w/Parmesan-Romano cheese and herbs, mix, prepared** (Noodle-Roni Parmesano)	260
w/sour cream and cheese sauce, mix, prepared** (Noodle-Roni Romanoff)	362
w/Stroganoff sauce, see Meat Entrees, pages 41 and 137	

* *Approximately ¾ cup to 1 cup*
** *According to package directions*

SPAGHETTI: CANNED, FROZEN & MIXES

See also "Frozen Dinners," "Pasta, Dry" and pages 136-141

	CALORIES
w/hot dogs and tomato sauce, canned (Heinz Minute Meal), 1 cup	308
w/hot dogs and tomato sauce, canned (SpaghettiO's), 1 cup	269
w/ground beef and tomato sauce, canned (Chef Boy-Ar-Dee), 1 cup	261
w/ground beef and tomato sauce, canned (Franco-American), 1 cup	289
w/meat sauce, canned (Heinz), 8 oz.*	174
w/meat and tomato sauce, mix, prepared** (Chef Boy-Ar-Dee Dinner), 1 cup	251
with meatballs:	
and tomato sauce, canned (Buitoni), 1 cup	259
and tomato sauce, canned (Chef Boy-Ar-Dee), 1 cup	249
and tomato sauce, canned (Franco-American), 1 cup	260
and tomato sauce, canned (La Rosa), 1 cup	227
and tomato sauce, canned (Morton House), 1 cup	613
and tomato sauce, canned (SpaghettiO's), 1 cup	228
and tomato sauce, frozen (Banquet Buffet Supper), 8 oz.	331

spaghetti with meatballs, continued

and tomato sauce, mix, prepared** (Chef Boy-Ar-Dee Dinner), 1 cup	343
w/mushrooms and tomato sauce, mix, prepared** (Chef Boy-Ar-Dee Dinner), 1 cup	229
w/tomato sauce, canned (Buitoni Spaghetti Twists), 8 oz.*	198
w/tomato sauce, mix, prepared** (Golden Grain Spaghetti Italiano Dinner), 1 cup	274
with tomato-cheese sauce:	
canned (Chef Boy-Ar-Dee), 1 cup	180
canned (Franco-American), 1 cup	200
canned (Franco-American Italian Style), 1 cup	190
canned (Heinz), 1 cup	178
canned (SpaghettiO's), 1 cup	200

* *Approximately ¾ cup to 1 cup*
** *According to package directions*

LASAGNE, MANICOTTI & RAVIOLI, 8 ounces, except as noted

See also page 138

	CALORIES
lasagne:	
canned (Chef Boy-Ar-Dee Lasagna)	241
frozen (Buitoni)	340
frozen (Roman)	274
mix, prepared* (Chef Boy-Ar-Dee Dinner)	265
manicotti, frozen (Buitoni), 1 piece, as packaged	82
manicotti, frozen (Roman), 1 piece, as packaged	163
ravioli:	
beef, w/sauce, canned (Chef Boy-Ar-Dee)	210
cheese, w/sauce, canned (Buitoni)	229
cheese, w/sauce, canned (Chef Boy-Ar-Dee)	263
cheese, w/sauce, canned (La Rosa)	205
cheese, wo/sauce, frozen (Buitoni)	244
cheese, wo/sauce, frozen (Roman)	496
meat, w/sauce, canned (Buitoni)	287
meat, w/sauce, canned (La Rosa)	218
meat, wo/sauce, frozen (Buitoni Raviolettes)	336
meat, wo/sauce, frozen (Roman)	552

* *According to package directions*

RICE, cooked*, 1 cup

See also "Rice, Flavored"

	CALORIES
brown (Carolina)	200
brown (River)	200
brown (Water Maid)	200
white:	
long grain (Carolina)	184
long grain (Mahatma)	184
medium grain (River)	184
medium grain (Water Maid)	184
parboiled (Aunt Caroline)	188
parboiled (Uncle Ben's Converted)	168
precooked (Carolina)	184
precooked (Minute Rice)	195
precooked (Uncle Ben's Quick)	194

** According to package directions, without butter*

RICE, FLAVORED, 1 cup, except as noted

See also "Rice"

	CALORIES
beef, flavored:	
mix, prepared* (Uncle Ben's)	204
mix, prepared* (Village Inn)	250
w/cracked rice, mix, prepared* (Betty Crocker Rice Keryiki)	416
w/vermicelli, mix, prepared* (Minute Rice Rib Roast Mix)	298
w/vermicelli, mix, prepared* (Rice-A-Roni)	321
w/cheese sauce, mix, prepared* (Betty Crocker Rice Milanese)	344
w/cheese sauce and pimientos, frozen (Green Giant Rice Risotto)	272
w/cheese sauce and vermicelli, mix, prepared* (Rice-A-Roni)	290
chicken flavored:	
mix, prepared* (Uncle Ben's)	208
mix, prepared* (Village Inn)	250
w/crumb topping, mix, prepared* (Betty Crocker Rice Provence)	367
w/vermicelli, mix, prepared* (Minute Rice Drumstick Mix)	304
w/vermicelli, mix, prepared* (Rice-A-Roni)	321
curry, mix, prepared* (Uncle Ben's)	212
curry, mix, prepared* (Village Inn)	250

fried, Chinese, see "Chinese Foods," page 53
fried, Chinese-style, w/vermicelli, mix, prepared* (Rice-A-Roni) 374
ham flavored, w/vermicelli, mix, prepared* (Rice-A-Roni) 298
herb, mix, prepared* (Village Inn) 250
long grain white and wild:
  w/sauce, frozen (Green Giant) 228
  mix, prepared* (Carolina) 294
  mix, prepared* (Uncle Ben's) 200
  mix, prepared* (Village Inn) 250
Mexican, see "Mexican Foods," page 54
w/peas and mushrooms, in sauce, frozen (Green Giant Rice Medley) ...218
w/peppers and parsley, in sauce, frozen (Green Giant Rice Verdi) 135
pilaf, frozen (Green Giant) 240
pilaf, mix, prepared* (Uncle Ben's) 290
Spanish:
  canned (Heinz Minute Meal), 8¾-oz. can** 196
  canned (La Rosa) 152
  canned (Old El Paso) 194
  canned (Stokely-Van Camp) 184
  frozen (Green Giant) 160
  mix, prepared* (Minute Rice) 298
  mix, prepared* (Uncle Ben's) 230
  mix, prepared* (Village Inn) 250
  w/vermicelli, mix, prepared* (Rice-A-Roni) 235
turkey flavored, w/vermicelli, mix, prepared* (Rice-A-Roni) 364
wild, w/vermicelli, mix, prepared* (Rice-A-Roni) 267
yellow, mix, prepared* (Village Inn) 250

** According to package directions*
*** Approximately 1 cup*

FATS, OILS AND SALAD DRESSINGS

11

FATS & OILS, 1 tablespoon

	CALORIES
butter (Meadow Gold)	100
butter (Sealtest)	102
margarine:	
(Blue Bonnet)	100
(Blue Bonnet Soft)	100
(Borden's Danish)	103
(Chiffon Soft)	96
(Fleischmann's)	100
(Fleischmann's Soft)	100
(Golden Glow)	105
(Good Luck)	105
(Imperial)	105
(Imperial Sof-Spread)	105
(Mazola)	100
(Mother's)	100
(Mother's Soft)	100
(Nucoa)	100
(Parkay)	101
(Sealtest)	102
liquid (Chiffon)	96
oil:	
corn (Mazola)	125
olive (Filippo Berio)	125
peanut (Planters)	125
vegetable (Crisco)	126
vegetable (Wesson)	125
shortening (Crisco)	103
shortening (Snowdrift)	102
shortening (Spry)	97

SALAD DRESSINGS, 1 tablespoon

See also page 148

	CALORIES
all-purpose, bottled (Lawry's)	59
bacon, mix, prepared* (Lawry's)	78
blue cheese:	
bottled (Kraft Roka Brand)	58
bottled (Lawry's)	57
mix, prepared* (Good Seasons)	85
mix, prepared* (Lawry's)	62
(Brockles Special)	93
Caesar, bottled (Lawry's)	70
Caesar, bottled (Seven Seas)	71
Canadian, bottled (Lawry's)	72
Coach House, bottled (Seven Seas)	78
cheese-garlic, mix, prepared* (Good Seasons)	85
cheese-Italian, mix, prepared* (Lawry's Italia)	84
cole slaw, bottled (Kraft),	62
French:	
bottled (Brockles)	54
bottled (Heinz)	78
bottled (Hellmann's)	70
bottled (Hellmann's Old Homestead)	70
bottled (Kraft)	67
bottled (Kraft Casino)	72
bottled (Kraft Catalina)	67
bottled (Kraft Miracle)	66
bottled (Wishbone Deluxe)	60
bottled (Wishbone Monaco)	74
mix, prepared* (Good Seasons Old Fashion)	84
mix, prepared* (Lawry's Old Fashion)	84
creamy, bottled (Seven Seas)	63
creamy, mix, prepared* (Good Seasons)	76
garlic, mix, prepared* (Good Seasons)	84
garlic-cheese, mix, prepared* (Lawry's)	84
garlic-French, bottled (Wishbone)	69
garlic-French, mix, prepared* (Lawry's)	83
green goddess, bottled (Lawry's)	59
green goddess, bottled (Seven Seas)	69
green goddess, bottled (Wishbone)	81

Hawaiian, bottled (Lawry's) 77
herb and garlic, bottled (Kraft) 83
Italian:
  bottled (Hellmann's) 85
  bottled (Kraft) 87
  bottled (Kraft Imperial) 62
  bottled (Seven Seas) 81
  bottled (Wishbone) 85
  bottled (Wishbone Golden) 45
  mix, prepared* (Good Seasons) 84
  mix, prepared* (Lawry's) 82
  creamy, bottled (Seven Seas) 81
  w/cheese, bottled (Lawry's) 60
  w/blue cheese, bottled (Seven Seas) 69
mayonnaise, bottled (Best Foods) 100
mayonnaise, bottled (Hellmann's) 100
mayonnaise, bottled (Kraft) 98
mayonnaise, bottled (Wesson) 97
mayonnaise-type, bottled (Heinz) 63
mayonnaise-type, bottled (Kraft Miracle Whip) 65
oil and vinegar, bottled (Kraft) 62
onion, mix, prepared* (Good Seasons) 84
onion, creamy, bottled (Wishbone) 40
onion, green, mix, prepared* (Lawry's) 84
Parmesan, mix, prepared* (Good Seasons) 84
Roquefort, bottled (Kraft) 58
Russian, bottled (Kraft) 65
Russian, bottled (Wishbone) 56
Russian, creamy, bottled (Seven Seas) 72
Russian, creamy, mix, prepared* (Good Seasons) 77
salad dressing, see "mayonnaise-type," above
Sea Island, bottled (Kraft) 93
sherry, bottled (Lawry's) 55
Tahitian Isle (Wishbone) 56
Thousand Island, bottled (Kraft) 73
Thousand Island, bottled (Wishbone) 65
tomato-blue cheese, bottled (Kraft Salad Secret) 52
tomato-spice, bottled (Seven Seas) 46

* *According to package directions*

CONDIMENTS, SAUCES AND RELATED PRODUCTS 12

CONDIMENTS & SEASONINGS, 1 tablespoon, except as noted

See also "Sauces," "Seasoning Mixes, Dry Form" and page 152

The caloric content of most herbs, spices, and seasonings is negligible; indeed, in many cases, nonexistent. For example, plain salt and pepper are calorie-free, and you'd have to use a bushel basket of most dried herbs—rosemary, thyme, dill, oregano, tarragon, etc. —to count them on your diet. If you're not accustomed to cooking with herbs and spices, now is a perfect time to experiment. Add new flavor to your food; take the doldrums out of dieting!

	CALORIES
capers (Crosse & Blackwell)	6
catsup:	
(Heinz)	16
(Hunt's)	18
(Hunt's Steak House)	18
(Smucker's)	31
(Stokely-Van Camp)	21
hot (Heinz)	21
celery flakes, dehydrated (Wyler's), 1 tsp.	7
celery salt, see "salt, flavored," page 66	
chili sauce (Heinz)	17
chili sauce (Hunt's)	18
chutney, Major Grey's (Crosse & Blackwell)	53
cocktail sauce (Crosse & Blackwell)	22
cocktail sauce (Tastee)	25
curry powder (Crosse & Blackwell)	26
(Durkee's Famous Sauce)	60
garlic flavoring, oil-base liquid (Burton's), ½ tsp.	21
garlic powder (Wyler's), ¼ tsp.	2
garlic salt, see "salt, flavored," page 66	

garlic spread, prepared* (Lawry's) 88
(Gravymaster), 2 tsp. 17
horseradish:
(Borden's) 16
(Kraft) 4
(Tastee Hot Tang) 5
cream style (Kraft) 5
oil style (Kraft) 5
dehydrated (Heinz) 26
hot sauce (Gebhardt), ¼ tsp. .... trace
hot sauce (Tabasco), ¼ tsp. .... trace
(Maggi Seasoning) 17
mayonnaise, see "Salad Dressings," page 63
mayonnaise-type salad dressing, see "Salad Dressings," page 63
meat sauce (Escoffier Sauce Robert) 19
meat sauce, sweet and sour (Heinz Savory Sauce) 21
meat sauce, sweet and spicy (H.P.) 21
meat-fish sauce (A.1.) 16
meat-fish sauce (Crosse & Blackwell) 21
meat-fish sauce (Escoffier Sauce Diable) 19
meat-fish sauce (Heinz 57) 14
mint sauce (Crosse & Blackwell) 16
mustard:
brown (Gulden's Spicy Brown) 13
brown (Heinz) 11
German-style (Kraft Dusseldorf) 15
hot (Grey Poupon) 13
hot (Gulden's Diablo) 13
hot (Heinz) 11
yellow (French's) 11
yellow (Gulden's) 11
yellow (Heinz) 10
yellow (Kraft) 12
w/horseradish (Kraft) 15
onion flakes, dehydrated (Wyler's), 1 tsp. 7
onion flavoring, oil-base liquid (Burton's), ½ tsp. 21
onion powder (Wyler's), ½ tsp. .... trace
onion salt, see "salt, flavored," page 66
onions, minced, instant, dehydrated (Borden's), 1 tsp. 7
onions, minced, instant, dehydrated (Wyler's), 1 tsp. 7
parsley flakes, dehydrated (Wyler's), 1 tsp. 1
pepper, seasoned (Lawry's), ½ tsp. 8

condiments and seasonings, continued

peppers, sweet, dehydrated (Wyler's), 1 tsp. 2

salt, flavored:

celery (Wyler's), ½ tsp. 4

garlic (Lawry's), ½ tsp. 3

garlic (Wyler's), ½ tsp. 3

onion (Wyler's), ½ tsp. 4

seasoned (Lawry's), ½ tsp. 6

sandwich spread (Hellmann's) 60

sandwich spread (Kraft Miracle) 56

soy sauce (La Choy) 6

taco sauce (Gebhardt), ½ oz. 3

tartar sauce (Hellmann's) 75

tartar sauce (Kraft) 72

tartar sauce, mix, prepared* (Lawry's) 67

vinegar, all varieties (Heinz) 3

Worcestershire sauce (Crosse & Blackwell) 15

Worcestershire sauce (Heinz) 11

Worcestershire sauce (Lea & Perrins) 12

* *According to package directions*

SAUCES, ½ cup, except as noted

See also "Condiments & Seasonings," "Gravies" and page 150

CALORIES

barbecue:

bottled (Cris 'N Pitt's) 120

bottled (Open Pit) 203

mix, prepared w/vinegar* (Durkee) 64

buttered, canned (Gebhardt), 4 oz. 72

chili, canned (Gebhardt), 4 oz. 56

garlic flavored, bottled (Cris 'N Pitt's) 120

garlic flavored, bottled (Open Pit) 203

hickory smoke flavored, bottled (Cris 'N Pitt's) 120

hickory smoke flavored, bottled (Open Pit) 203

hickory smoke flavored, bottled (Heinz) 160

hot, bottled (Cris 'N Pitts) 120

w/onion bits, bottled (Heinz) 144

Béarnaise, in jars (Butternut Farm) 176

Bordelaise, in jars (Butternut Farm) 48

cheese, mix, prepared* (Durkee) 144

cheese, mix, prepared* (French's) 120
cheese, mix, prepared* (McCormick) 154
chili hot dog, w/meat, canned (Gebhardt), 4 oz. 156
chili hot dog, mix, prepared wo/meat* (McCormick) 92
clam, red, canned (Buitoni) 102
clam, red, canned (La Rosa) 89
clam, white, canned (Buitoni) 114
clam, white, canned (La Rosa) 78
enchilada, canned (Gebhardt), 4 oz. 68
Hollandaise:
  in jars (Butternut Farm) 176
  in jars (Cresca) 156
  in jars (Lord Mott's) 114
  mix, prepared* (Durkee) 223
  mix, prepared* (French's) 129
pizza, canned (Buitoni) 79
pizza, canned (Contadina) 84
sour cream, mix, prepared* (Durkee) 162
sour cream, mix, prepared* (French's) 210
sour cream, mix, prepared* (McCormick) 146
spaghetti:
  canned (Buitoni) 88
  canned (Lambrecht), 4 oz. 72
  canned (La Rosa) 73
  in jars (Prince) 90
  mix, prepared wo/meat* (Durkee) 44
  mix, prepared* (French's) 89
  mix, prepared* (McCormick) 53
  mix, prepared w/oil* (Spatini) 50
  mix, prepared wo/oil* (Spatini) 25
  Marinara, canned (Buitoni) 84
  Marinara, canned (La Rosa) 74
  w/meat, canned (Buitoni) 138
  w/meat, canned (Franco-American) 120
  w/meat, in jars (Prince) 143
  w/mushrooms, canned (Buitoni) 94
  w/mushrooms, canned (Franco-American) 95
  w/mushrooms, in jars (Prince) 103
  w/mushrooms, mix, prepared* (French's) 71
  w/mushrooms, mix, prepared* (Lawry's) 116
tomato, canned (Contadina) 52
tomato, canned (Hunt's) 35
tomato, w/cheese, canned (Hunt's) 53

sauces, continued

tomato, w/mushrooms, canned (Hunt's)	42
tomato paste, see "Tomato Paste & Purée," page 37	
tomato purée, see "Tomato Paste & Purée," page 37	

* *According to package directions*

GRAVIES, ½ cup

See also "Condiments & Seasonings," "Sauces" and page 150

	CALORIES
beef, canned (Franco-American)	95
beef, canned (Ready Gravy)	84
beef, brown, canned (Howard Johnson's)	80
beef, mix, prepared* (Wyler's)	48
brown, mix, prepared* (Durkee)	48
brown, mix, prepared* (French's)	36
brown, mix, prepared* (McCormick)	59
brown, mix, prepared w/butter* (Lawry's)	118
chicken giblet, canned (Franco-American)	56
chicken:	
canned (College Inn)	49
canned (Franco-American)	107
mix, prepared* (Durkee)	32
mix, prepared* (French's)	63
mix, prepared* (McCormick)	48
mix, prepared* (Wyler's)	48
herb, mix, prepared* (McCormick)	51
mushroom:	
canned (Franco-American)	60
mix, prepared* (Durkee)	32
mix, prepared* (French's)	32
mix, prepared* (McCormick)	40
mix, prepared* (Wyler's)	30
mix, prepared w/butter* (Lawry's)	122
mustard, mix, prepared* (French's)	32
onion, mix, prepared* (Durkee)	48
onion, mix, prepared* (French's)	36
onion, mix, prepared* (McCormick)	51
onion, mix, prepared* (Wyler's)	34
turkey giblet, canned (Howard Johnson's)	80

* *According to package directions*

SEASONING MIXES, DRY FORM

See also "Gravies" and "Sauces"

The only way you can be sure of the caloric content of most foods prepared with a seasoning mix is to total the calories in the mix with the calories in all other ingredients used. Most package recipes simply aren't specific enough to permit listing the finished food, prepared "according to package directions." For instance, a recipe may call for "1 pound ground meat," but only you can know if you use a pound of "regular" ground beef (about 1216 calories) or a pound of lean ground beef (about 812 calories)!

	CALORIES
à la king (Durkee), 2-oz. pkg.	297
beef goulash (Lawry's), 1⅔-oz. pkg.	127
beef stew (French's), 1⅞-oz. pkg.	133
beef stew (Lawry's), 1⅝-oz. pkg.	131
beef stew (McCormick), 1½-oz. pkg.	90
beef Stroganoff (French's), 1¾-oz. pkg.	192
beef Stroganoff (Lawry's), 1½-oz. pkg.	118
beef Stroganoff (McCormick), 1½-oz. pkg.	113
chili con carne (Durkee), 2¼-oz. pkg.	196
chili con carne (French's Chili-O), 1¾-oz. pkg.	123
chili con carne (Lawry's), 1⅝-oz. pkg.	137
enchilada (Lawry's), 1⅝-oz. pkg.	144
enchilada (McCormick), 1½-oz. pkg.	113
ground beef, w/onions (French's), 1⅛-oz. pkg.	79
hamburger and meat loaf (McCormick), 1½-oz. pkg.	119
meat loaf (Lawry's), 3½-oz. pkg.	333
onion burger (McCormick), 1-oz. pkg.	86
Sloppy Joe:	
(Durkee), 1½-oz. pkg.	119
(French's), 1½-oz. pkg.	116
(Lawry's), 1½-oz. pkg.	139
(McCormick), 1 5/16-oz. pkg.	102
Spanish rice (Lawry's), 1½-oz. pkg.	125
Swiss steak (McCormick), 1-oz. pkg.	44
taco (French's), 1¾-oz. pkg.	123
taco (Lawry's), 1¼-oz. pkg.	120
tuna casserole (McCormick), 1½-oz. pkg.	104

PUDDINGS, CUSTARDS AND GELATIN PRODUCTS 13

PUDDINGS, PIE FILLINGS & CUSTARDS, ½ cup, except as noted

See also "Gelatin Salad-Desserts" and pages 153 and 157

Bear in mind that you can reduce the calories in made-with-milk puddings by substituting skim milk for whole milk. Depending on the fat content of the skim milk you use, you'll save 50 to 80 calories whenever you substitute one cup of skim milk for one cup of whole milk. For example, most cooking and instant mix puddings call for two cups of milk. By using two cups of skim milk, you'll save 100 to 160 calories—the equivalent of 25 to 40 calories per half cup serving!

	CALORIES
banana, mix, prepared* (Shake-A-Pudd'n)	165
banana, cooking mix, prepared* (Royal)	165
banana cream, cooking mix, prepared* (Jell-O)	173
banana cream, cooking mix, prepared* (My-T-Fine)	175
banana cream, instant mix, prepared* (Jell-O)	178
banana cream, instant mix, prepared* (Royal)	175
Bavarian cream, cooking mix, prepared* (My-T-Fine)	175
butter pecan, cooking mix, prepared* (My-T-Fine)	177
butterscotch:	
cooking mix, prepared* (Foremost)	175
cooking mix, prepared* (Jell-O)	173
cooking mix, prepared* (My-T-Fine)	171
cooking mix, prepared* (Royal)	190
instant mix, prepared* (Jell-O)	178
instant mix, prepared* (Royal)	185
caramel-nut, instant mix, prepared* (Royal)	195
cherry, mix, prepared* (Whip 'n Chill)	139
cherry-plum, mix, prepared* (Junket Danish Dessert)	135
chocolate:	
canned (Bounty Dutch)	174

dairy-packed (Dannon Bokoo) 150
mix, prepared* (Shake-A-Pudd'n) 200
mix, prepared* (Whip 'n Chill) 144
cooking mix, prepared* (Foremost) 175
cooking mix, prepared* (Jell-O) 175
cooking mix, prepared* (My-T-Fine) 187
cooking mix, prepared* (Royal) 190
cooking mix, prepared* (Royal Dark 'N Sweet) 195
instant mix, prepared* (Jell-O) 191
instant mix, prepared* (Royal) 200
instant mix, prepared* (Royal Dark 'N Sweet) 200
chocolate almond, cooking mix, prepared* (My-T-Fine) 196
chocolate fudge:
mix, prepared* (Whip 'n Chill) 139
cooking mix, prepared* (Foremost) 175
cooking mix, prepared* (Jell-O) 175
cooking mix, prepared* (My-T-Fine) 190
instant mix, prepared* (Jell-O) 191
chocolate malt, mix, prepared* (Shak-A-Pudd'n) 200
coconut, toasted, instant mix, prepared* (Royal) 185
coconut cream, cooking mix, prepared* (Jell-O) 175
coconut cream, instant mix, prepared* (Jell-O) 189
currant-raspberry, mix, prepared* (Junket Danish Dessert) 135
custard:
cooking mix, prepared* (Royal) 145
Bavarian, cooking mix, prepared* (Rice-A-Roni) 124
egg, cooking mix, prepared** (Jell-O) 165
egg, caramel, cooking mix, prepared* (My-T-Fine) 145
egg, vanilla, cooking mix, prepared* (My-T-Fine) 156
rennet, all flavors except chocolate, mix, prepared* (Junket) 132
rennet, chocolate, mix, prepared* (Junket) 147
Indian, canned (B & M) 150
Junket, see "custard, rennet," above
lemon:
canned (Bounty) 196
mix, prepared* (Whip 'n Chill) 135
cooking mix, prepared* (Foremost) 197
cooking mix, prepared* (Jell-O) 178
cooking mix, prepared* (My-T-Fine) 180
instant mix, prepared* (Jell-O) 178
instant mix, prepared* (Royal) 180
lemon chiffon, cooking mix, prepared* (Jell-O) 144

puddings, pie fillings and custards, continued

mocha-nut, instant mix, prepared* (Royal) 190
pineapple cream, cooking mix, prepared* (Jell-O) 168
pineapple cream, instant mix, prepared* (Jell-O) 178
pistachio nut, instant mix, prepared* (Royal) 180
plum, canned (Crosse & Blackwell), 4-oz. serving 340
rice, canned (Bounty) 193
strawberry, mix, prepared* (Junket Danish Dessert) 135
strawberry, mix, prepared* (Shak-A-Pudd'n) 160
strawberry, mix, prepared* (Whip 'n Chill) 135
tapioca:
  chocolate, mix, prepared* (Jell-O) 166
  chocolate, mix, prepared* (Royal) 185
  lemon, mix, prepared* (Jell-O) 166
  orange, mix, prepared* (Jell-O) 166
  vanilla, mix, prepared* (Jell-O) 166
  vanilla, mix, prepared* (My-T-Fine) 144
  vanilla, mix, prepared* (Royal) 170
vanilla:
  canned (Bounty French) 128
  dairy-packed (Dannon Bokoo French) 150
  mix, prepared* (Shake-A-Pudd'n) 165
  mix, prepared* (Whip 'n Chill) 135
  cooking mix, prepared* (Foremost) 175
  cooking mix, prepared* (Jell-O) 164
  cooking mix, prepared* (My-T-Fine) 171
  cooking mix, prepared* (Royal) 165
  instant mix, prepared* (Jell-O) 178
  instant mix, prepared* (Royal) 180

** According to package directions, with whole fresh milk whenever milk is called for*
*** According to package directions, without egg yolk*

GELATIN, UNFLAVORED

CALORIES

dry (Knox), 1 envelope 28

GELATIN SALAD-DESSERTS, ½ cup

See also "Puddings, Pie Fillings & Custards"

CALORIES

all flavors, mix, prepared* (Jell-O) 81

all flavors, mix, prepared* (Jell-O 1-2-3) 101
all flavors, mix, prepared* (Jells Best) 77
all flavors, mix, prepared* (Royal) 80
cherry, dairy-packed (Borden's) 94
fruit cocktail, dairy-packed (Borden's) 109
mandarin orange, dairy-packed (Borden's) 89
perfection, dairy-packed (Borden's) 81
pineapple-papaya, dairy-packed (Borden's) 78
raspberry-pineapple, dairy-packed (Borden's) 78
strawberry, dairy-packed (Borden's) 75

* *According to package directions*

CAKES, COOKIES, PIES AND OTHER BAKED GOODS 14

CAKES, FROZEN

See also "Cake Mixes," "Specialty Snack Cakes" and pages 158-161

	CALORIES
chocolate, frosted (Pepperidge Farm), whole cake*	1920
chocolate, frosted (Pepperidge Farm), 1 slice**	240
chocolate fudge, frosted:	
(Howard Johnson's), whole cake*	1785
(Howard Johnson's), 1 slice**	223
(Pepperidge Farm), whole cake*	1890
(Pepperidge Farm), 1 slice**	236
coconut, frosted (Howard Johnson's), whole cake*	1615
coconut, frosted (Howard Johnson's), 1 slice**	202
cream cheese (Lambrecht), whole cake*	1530
cream cheese (Lambrecht), 1 slice**	191
devil's food, frosted (Pepperidge Farm), whole cake*	1956
devil's food, frosted (Pepperidge Farm), 1 slice**	245
orange, frosted (Howard Johnson's), whole cake*	1700
orange, frosted (Howard Johnson's), 1 slice**	213
vanilla, frosted (Pepperidge Farm) whole cake*	1986
vanilla, frosted (Pepperidge Farm), 1 slice**	248

** 17 ounces*
*** 1/8 of whole cake, inner slice*

CAKE MIXES, PREPARED*

See also "Cakes, Frozen," "Specialty Snack Cakes," pages 158-161

	CALORIES
angel food:	
(Duncan Hines), whole cake	2004
(Duncan Hines), 1 slice**	167
(Swans Down), whole cake	1590
(Swans Down), 1 slice**	133

cheesecake:
no-bake (Jell-O), whole cake 2040
no-bake (Jell-O), 1 slice** 170
no-bake (Royal), whole cake 1880
no-bake (Royal), 1 slice** 156
chocolate (Swans Down German), whole cake 2242
chocolate (Swans Down German), 1 slice** 188
coffeecake, w/topping (Aunt Jemima), whole cake 1450
coffeecake, w/topping (Aunt Jemima), 1 slice† 242
devil's food:
(Duncan Hines), whole cake 2460
(Duncan Hines), 1 slice** 205
(Swans Down), whole cake 2232
(Swans Down), 1 slice** 187
white:
(Duncan Hines), whole cake 2220
(Duncan Hines), 1 slice** 185
(Swans Down), whole cake 2124
(Swans Down), 1 slice** 178
yellow:
(Duncan Hines), whole cake 2400
(Duncan Hines), 1 slice** 200
(Swans Down), whole cake 2244
(Swans Down), 1 slice** 188

** According to package directions, without icing or topping except as noted*
*** 1/12 of whole cake*
† 1/6 of whole cake

SPECIALTY SNACK CAKES*

See also "Cakes, Frozen," "Cake Mixes," and pages 158-161

CALORIES

chocolate, creme filled (Drake's Yankee Doodles), 1-oz. cake 124
devil's food, creme filled:
(Hostess Suzy Q's), 1¼-oz. cake 141
chocolate coated (Drake's Yodel's), ⅞-oz. roll 134
chocolate coated (Hostess Big Wheels), 1⅜-oz. cake 167
chocolate coated (Hostess Big Wheels), 1⅓-oz. cake** 162
chocolate coated (Hostess Ding Dongs—dark), 1⅜-oz. cake 168
chocolate coated (Hostess Ding Dongs—milk), 1⅜-oz. cake 167
chocolate coated (Hostess Ding Dongs—milk), 1½-oz. cake† 182
chocolate coated (Hostess Ho Ho's), ⅞-oz. roll 111

devil's food, creme filled, continued

chocolate coated (Hostess Ho Ho's), 9/10-oz. cake† 114
chocolate topped (Hostess Cupcakes), 1½-oz. cake 145
chocolate topped (Hostess Cupcakes), 1⅙-oz. cake** 112
coconut coated (Hostess Sno Balls), 1¼-oz. cake 115
orange, creme filled topped (Hostess Cupcakes), 1½-oz. cake 154
orange, creme filled, topped (Hostess Cupcakes), 1⅙-oz. cake** 119
yellow, creme filled (Drake's Golden Creme Cups), 1⅜-oz. cake 172
yellow, creme filled (Hostess Twinkies), 1⅜-oz. cake 133
yellow, creme filled (Hostess Twinkies), 1⅓-oz. cake** 129

* *Note variations in size*
** *From 12-cake carton*
† *From 10-cake carton*

COOKIES, 1 piece, as packaged

See also "Miscellaneous Baked Products" and page 161

Bear in mind that cookies are available in dozens of sizes and shapes; therefore, it is hard—indeed, just about impossible—to accurately compare the caloric content of different brands and types. (See "How to Use This Book," pages xv-xviii.)

CALORIES

almond (Keebler Jan Hagel) 47
almond (Stella D'Oro Almond Toast) 49
almond-spice (Keebler Dutch Almond) 51
animal crackers:
(Keebler) 12
(Nabisco Barnum's) 12
(Sunshine) 10
iced (Keebler Party) 52
anise flavored (Stella D'Oro Anisette Sponge) 50
anise flavored (Stella D'Oro Anisette Toast) 34
apple flavored (Keebler Dutch Apple) 27
apple flavored (Nabisco Apple Strudel) 48
applesauce (Sunshine) 33
applesauce, iced (Sunshine) 104
arrowroot (Nabisco National) 22
arrowroot (Sunshine) 15
brown edge (Nabisco Wafers) 28
brown sugar (Nabisco Family Favorite) 25
butter flavored:
(Keebler Old Fashioned) 84

(Nabisco Old Fashioned) 30
(Sunshine—large) 32
(Sunshine—small) 14
(Zu Zu) 16
graham crackers:
(Keebler Honey) 17
(Keebler Thin) 17
(Keebler Very Thin) 14
(Nabisco) 30
(Nabisco Honeymaid) 30
(Sunshine) 17
(Sunshine Sugar Honey) 30
chocolate covered (Keebler Deluxe) 44
chocolate covered (Milco Dandies) 91
chocolate covered (Nabisco) 55
chocolate covered (Nabisco Fancy) 68
chocolate covered (Pantry) 62
chocolate covered (Robena) 72
kichel (Stella D'Oro Old Country Treats) 64
lemon (Keebler Old Fashioned) 83
lemon (Nabisco Snaps) 17
lemon-nut (Pepperidge Farm Crunch) 58
macaroons:
(Sunshine) 85
butter flavored (Sunshine) 39
coconut (Bake Shop) 87
coconut (Sunshine) 81
sandwich (Nabisco) 71
marshmallow:
chocolate covered (Keebler Chocolate Dainties) 68
chocolate covered (Keebler Chocolate Treasures) 83
chocolate covered (Keebler Galaxies) 82
chocolate covered (Keebler Tulips) 83
chocolate covered (Mallomars) 60
chocolate covered (Nabisco Puffs) 94
chocolate covered (Nabisco Twirls) 133
chocolate covered (Pinwheels) 139
chocolate covered (Sunshine Chocolate Puffs) 63
chocolate covered (Sunshine Kings) 135
iced (Sunshine Frosted Cakes) 68
iced (Sunshine Nut Sundae) 74
sandwich (Nabisco) 32

marshmallow, continued

sandwich (Keebler Mellow) 81
w/chocolate sprinkles (Sunshine Sprinkles) 71
w/coconut (Nabisco Fancy Crests) 54
w/coconut (Sunshine Mallo Puffs) 70

oatmeal:

(Keebler Old Fashioned) 78
(Nabisco Family Favorite) 24
(Nabisco Home Style) 61
(Sunshine) 60
iced (Keebler) 82
w/whole raisins (Bake Shop) 76
w/whole raisins (Pepperidge Farm) 54

peach-apricot (Stella D'Oro Pastry) 99
peanut (Sunshine) 33
peanut, chocolate covered (Ideal) 94
peanut butter (Sunshine Crunch) 68
peanut butter (Sunshine Patties) 30
peanut butter, chocolate covered (Eton Stix) 53
peanut butter, chocolate covered (Keebler Penguin) 117
peanut caramel (Hey Days) 122
peanut cream (Nabisco Patties) 34
pecan (Keebler Crisp) 20
pecan (Sunshine Crunch) 78
(Pitter Patter Sandwich) 86
prune (Stella D'Oro Pastry) 87
raisin (Nabisco Fruit Biscuit) 56
raisin (Stella D'Oro Golden Bars) 115
raisin (Sunshine Golden Fruit) 73
raisin, iced (Keebler Bars) 81
sesame (Stella D'Oro Regina) 48

shortbread:

(Keebler Buttercup) 27
(Lorna Doone) 38
(Scottie) 39
cashew (Nabisco Home Style) 50
chocolate covered (Nabisco Striped) 50
coconut, iced (Keebler) 65
iced (Keebler Fudge Stripes) 58
pecan (Keebler Sandies) 84
pecan (Nabisco) 77

(Social Tea Biscuits) 21
sugar (Eton) 50

sugar (Keebler Giant) 70
sugar (Keebler Old Fashioned) 81
sugar (Nabisco Snaps) 17
sugar wafers:
(Biscos) 18
(Biscos Creme Waffles) 47
(Sunshine Clover Leaves) 25
(Keebler—14-oz. pkg., all flavors) 31
(Keebler—7-oz. pkg., chocolate) 26
(Keebler—7-oz. pkg., strawberry) 25
(Keebler—7-oz. pkg., vanilla) 25
(Kreemlined) 45
(Regent) 23
(Sunshine) 47
chocolate covered (Eton Fudge Stix) 55
chocolate covered (Eton Peanut Butter Stix) 53
chocolate covered (Milco) 80
chocolate covered (Nabisco) 76
chocolate covered (Nabisco Creme Stix) 50
chocolate covered (Sunshine Ice Box) 30
spiced (Nabisco) 33
(Swedish Kreme) 103
(Swiss Chalet) 97
vanilla (Keebler Wafers) 19
vanilla (Nabisco Snaps) 13
vanilla (Nabisco Wafers) 18
vanilla (Sunshine Wafers) 14

PIES & PASTRIES

See also pages 154 and 160-161

CALORIES

pies, fruit and custard varieties:
all flavors (Hostess), 4¾-oz. "individual" pie 435
apple, frozen (Banquet), whole pie* 1400
apple, frozen (Banquet), 1 slice** 175
apple, frozen (Morton), whole pie* 1440
apple, frozen (Morton), 1 slice** 180
blueberry, frozen (Banquet), whole pie* 1464
blueberry, frozen (Banquet), 1 slice** 183
boysenberry, frozen (Banquet), whole pie* 1372
boysenberry, frozen (Banquet), 1 slice** 172

pies, fruit and custard varieties, continued

cherry, frozen (Banquet), whole pie* 1408
cherry, frozen (Banquet), 1 slice** 176
cherry, frozen (Morton), whole pie* 1498
cherry, frozen (Morton), 1 slice** 187
coconut custard, frozen (Banquet), whole pie* 1176
coconut custard, frozen (Banquet), 1 slice** 147
custard, frozen (Banquet), whole pie* 1088
custard, frozen (Banquet), 1 slice** 136
mincemeat, frozen (Banquet), whole pie* 1604
mincemeat, frozen (Banquet), 1 slice** 201
peach, frozen (Banquet), whole pie* 1276
peach, frozen (Banquet), 1 slice** 160
pumpkin (Banquet), whole pie* 1208
pumpkin (Banquet), 1 slice** 151

pies, cream varieties, frozen:

banana cream (Banquet), 14-oz. whole pie 1036
banana cream (Banquet), 1 slice† 173
butterscotch cream (Banquet), 14-oz. whole pie 1081
butterscotch cream (Banquet), 1 slice† 180
chocolate cream (Banquet), 14-oz. whole pie 1131
chocolate cream (Banquet), 1 slice† 189
chocolate cream (Morton), 14-oz. whole pie 1030
chocolate cream (Morton), 1 slice† 171
coconut cream (Banquet), 14-oz. whole pie 1170
coconut cream (Banquet), 1 slice† 195
cream cheese, see "cream cheese cake," page 74
Key lime cream (Banquet), 14-oz. whole pie 1142
Key lime cream (Banquet), 1 slice† 190
lemon cream (Banquet), 14-oz. whole pie 1002
lemon cream (Banquet), 1 slice† 167
Neapolitan cream (Banquet), 14-oz. whole pie 1053
Neapolitan cream (Banquet), 1 slice† 176
strawberry cream (Banquet), 14-oz. whole pie 1047
strawberry cream (Banquet), 1 slice† 175
strawberry cream (Morton), 14-oz. whole pie 987
strawberry cream (Morton), 1 slice† 165

pies, no-bake mixes, prepared‡:

cheesecake, see "Cake Mixes, Prepared," page 75
chocolate (Royal Dutch), whole pie 2040
chocolate (Royal Dutch), 1 slice** 255
devil cream (Royal), whole pie 2280
devil cream (Royal), 1 slice** 285

lemon (Royal Lemon Confetti), whole pie 2080
lemon (Royal Lemon Confetti), 1 slice** 260
Nesselrode (Royal), whole pie 2000
Nesselrode (Royal), 1 slice** 250
spumoni (Royal), whole pie 2120
spumoni (Royal), 1 slice** 265

strudels, frozen:
apple (Pepperidge Farm), 14-oz. whole strudel 1215
apple (Pepperidge Farm), 1 slice† 203
blueberry (Pepperidge Farm), 14-oz. whole strudel 1278
blueberry (Pepperidge Farm), 1 slice† 213

turnovers, frozen:
apple (Pepperidge Farm), 3-oz. turnover 315
blueberry (Pepperidge Farm), 3-oz. turnover 321
cherry (Pepperidge Farm), 3-oz. turnover 342

** 20 ounces*
*** 1/8 of whole pie*
† 1/6 of whole pie or strudel
‡ According to package directions

PASTRY SHELLS & PIE CRUST

CALORIES

pastry shells (Stella D'Oro), 1 shell, as packaged 146
pastry shells, frozen (Pepperidge Farm Patty Shells),
1 shell, as packaged 232
pie crust, mix, prepared*
(Flako), single 9" crust 738

** According to package directions*

MISCELLANEOUS BAKED PRODUCTS

CALORIES

brownies, nut fudge (Bake Shop), 1 brownie* 264
brownies, pecan fudge (Keebler), 1 brownie* 260
cinnamon sticks, frozen (Quaker), 1 stick* 49
corn bread, mix, prepared** (Aunt Jemima),
2¾" x 2⅝" x 1¼" slice 224
corn sticks, frozen (Quaker), 1 stick* 57
doughnuts, powdered, frozen (Morton Donuts), 1 doughnut* 82
doughnuts, sugar and spice, frozen (Morton Donuts), I doughnut* 82
gingerbread, mix, prepared** (Dromedary), 1" x 4" piece 100

toaster pastries, 1 tart†:
- all flavors (Toast 'Em Danka Danish), 1½ oz. 210
- all flavors (Toast 'Em Pop-Ups), 1¾ oz. 181
- all flavors (Kellogg's Danish Go-Rounds), 2 oz. 236
- all fruit flavors (Kellogg's Pop-Tarts), 1.8 oz. 203
- all fruit frosted flavors (Kellogg's Pop-Tarts), 1.8 oz. 207
- apple (Nabisco Toastettes), 1¾ oz. 197
- blueberry (Nabisco Toastettes), 1¾ oz. 199
- brown sugar-cinnamon (Kellogg's Pop-Tarts), 1.8 oz. 209
- brown sugar-cinnamon (Nabisco Toastettes), 1¾ oz. 193
- cherry (Nabisco Toastettes), 1¾ oz. 196
- chocolate, frosted (Kellogg's Pop-Tarts), 1.8 oz. 240
- strawberry (Nabisco Toastettes), 1¾ oz. 198

* *As packaged*
** *According to package directions*
† *Note variations in size*

JELLIES, PRESERVES, SYRUPS, TOPPINGS AND RELATED PRODUCTS

15

JELLIES & PRESERVES, 1 tablespoon, except as noted

See also page 163

	CALORIES
butter, apple (Smucker's)	39
butter, peach (Smucker's)	47
jelly:	
all flavors (Crosse & Blackwell)	51
all flavors (Kraft)	46
all flavors (Ma Brown)	49
all flavors (Smucker's)	49
grape (Welch's)	50
marmalade, orange (Crosse & Blackwell)	60
marmalade, orange (Kraft)	52
preserves:	
all flavors (Crosse & Blackwell)	59
all flavors (Kraft)	52
all flavors (Ma Brown)	51
all flavors (Smucker's)	54
(Smucker's Dutch Girl)	28

SYRUPS, 1 tablespoon

See also "Dessert Toppings" and "Sweet Flavorings"

	CALORIES
chocolate flavored (Hershey's)	51
chocolate flavored (Kraft)	47
chocolate flavored (Smucker's)	58
corn (Karo, blue label)	60
corn (Karo, red label)	60

syrups, continued

maple, blended (Log Cabin) 52
maple, pure (Cary's) 55
maple flavored:
  (Aunt Jemima) 53
  (Happy Jack) 50
  (Karo) 60
  (Log Cabin's Country Kitchen) 50
  (Smucker's) 43
  (Vermont Maid) 47
  buttered (Log Cabin) 54
maple-honey flavored (Log Cabin) 50
molasses, blackstrap (Brer Rabbit) 53
molasses, light (Brer Rabbit) 60

DESSERT TOPPINGS, 1 tablespoon

See also "Syrups"

CALORIES

butterscotch (Hershey's) 55
butterscotch (Kraft) 55
butterscotch (Smucker's) 64
caramel, chocolate (Kraft) 54
caramel, vanilla (Kraft) 57
caramel, vanilla (Smucker's) 66
chocolate flavor mint (Hershey's) 61
chocolate flavor peanut butter (Hershey's) 61
chocolate fudge (Hershey's) 60
chocolate fudge (Kraft) 46
chocolate fudge (Smucker's) 66
cream, whipped, aerosol canned (Reddi-Wip) 8
cream, whipped, aerosol canned (Top-Wip) 7
hard sauce (Crosse & Blackwell) 64
marshmallow creme (Kraft) 21
pecans, in syrup (Kraft) 82
pecans, in syrup (Smucker's) 73
pineapple (Kraft) 56
pineapple (Smucker's) 55
spoonmallow (Kraft) 33
strawberry (Kraft) 53
walnuts, in syrup (Kraft) 72
walnuts, in syrup (Smucker's) 71

whip, non-dairy:
- aerosol canned (Kraft) 9
- aerosol canned (Lucky Whip) 11
- aerosol canned (Reddi-Wip) 9
- frozen (Cool Whip) 16
- frozen (Pet) 16
- mix, prepared* (Dream Whip) 14
- mix, prepared* (Lucky Whip) 10

* *According to package directions*

SWEET FLAVORINGS, 1 teaspoon

	CALORIES
cherry extract (Burton's)	9
coffee (Burnett's)	9
grenadine (Garnier)	17
grenadine (Holland House)	15
orgeat (Garnier)	17
peppermint extract (Burnett's)	12
pineapple, pure (Burton's)	12
raspberry, imitation (Burton's)	10
raspberry, pure (Burton's)	8
rose extract (Burnett's)	9
rum, imitation (Burnett's)	11
strawberry, pure (Burton's)	10
vanilla extract, pure (Burnett's)	42
vanilla extract, imitation (Gold Medal)	trace

MISCELLANEOUS SWEET BAKING INGREDIENTS, 1 ounce

	CALORIES
butterscotch (Nestlé's Morsels)	150
chocolate:	
bitter (Hershey's Baking)	169
pre-melted (Nestlé's Choco-Bake)	172
semisweet (Baker's)	130
semisweet (Baker's Chips)	130
unsweetened (Baker's)	140
semisweet (Ghirardelli Chips)	146
semisweet (Hershey's)	147
semisweet (Nestlé's Morsels)	137

chocolate, continued

sweet (Baker's German) 130

coconut, flaked (Baker's Angel Flake) 150

coconut, grated (Baker's Fine Grated) 150

ginger, crystallized (Borden's Tropical) 97

ginger, preserved (Borden's Tropical) 88

CANDIES, ICE CREAM AND OTHER CONFECTIONS 16

CANDY, 1 ounce

See also page 164

See "How to Use This Book," pages xv-xviii to learn how to determine the number of ounces—and, therefore, the number of calories—in a specific candy bar, roll of hard candy, etc.

	CALORIES
(Butterfinger)	130
butter rum drops, see "hard candy," page 91	
butterscotch drops, see "hard candy," page 91	
caramel:	
chocolate or vanilla (Curtiss)	113
chocolate or vanilla (Kraft)	114
chocolate, w/nut slivers (Choclettos)	112
coconut (Kraft)	119
vanilla (Sugar Daddy)	113
walnut, w/nut slivers (Walnettos)	115
caramel, chocolate covered:	
coconut (Kraft)	124
vanilla (Kraft)	120
vanilla (Kraft Caramelettes)	121
vanilla (Milk Duds)	111
vanilla (Nestlé's Caramel Cream)	124
vanilla (Pom Poms)	119
vanilla (Sugar Babies)	113
w/nuts, see "nuts and caramel, chocolate covered," page 93	
cherries, dark chocolate covered (Welch's)	115
cherries, milk chocolate covered (Welch's)	108
cherry drops, see "hard candy," page 91, and "jellied candy," page 91	
chocolate, solid:	
milk (Ghirardelli—bars)	150
milk (Ghirardelli—blocks)	149

chocolate, solid, continued

- milk (Hershey's—bars) 152
- milk (Hershey's—blocks) 145
- milk (Hershey's Kisses) 152
- milk (Nestlé's) 148
- milk (Welch's Stars) 116
- mint (Ghirardelli) 150
- mint (Welch's Mint Wafers) 142
- semisweet (Eagle) 149
- semisweet (Hershey's) 147
- semisweet (Hershey's Dainties) 147
- semisweet (Nestlé's) 141
- semisweet (Nestlé's Morsels) 137
- sweet (Hershey's Pennsylvania Dutch) 145

chocolate, candy coated:

- milk (Hershey-Ets) 134
- mint (Hershey's) 133

chocolate, with fruit and/or nuts:

- w/almonds (Ghirardelli) 152
- w/almonds (Hershey's) 154
- w/almonds (Nestlé's) 149
- w/fruit and nuts (Chunky) 135
- w/fruit and nuts (Nestlé's Fruit 'N Nut) 140
- w/peanuts (Mr. Goodbar) 153
- w/pecans (Pecan Chunky) 135
- w/raisins (Ghirardelli) 142

chocolate, with crisps, chips and bits:

- w/butter toffee chips (Hershey's Butter Chip) 144
- w/crisped rice (Ghirardelli) 150
- w/crisped rice (Krackel) 148
- w/crisped rice (Nestlé's Crunch) 140
- w/malted milk bits (Welch's Crunch) 118
- w/malted milk bits and almond chips (Peter Paul Almond Cluster) .. 144

(Chocolate Babies) 155

(Chocolate Sponge) 122

coconut, chocolate covered:

- (Mason Peaks) 175
- (Moundettes) 126
- (Mounds) 125
- (Peter Paul) 126
- (Welch's) 132
- w/almonds (Almond Joy) 132
- w/almonds (Almond Joy Miniatures) 133

cinnamon drops, see "hard candy," page 91
coffee drops, see "hard candy," page 91
crisps, chocolate covered, w/caramel:
(Caravelle) 127
($100,000) 121
(Forever Yours) 98
fudge:
chocolate (Walter Johnson) 104
chocolate (Kraft Fudgies) 120
chocolate (Welch's Home Style) 105
chocolate, chocolate covered (Welch's) 122
chocolate, chocolate covered, w/nuts (Bonanza) 153
chocolate, chocolate covered, w/nuts (Welch's) 114
vanilla (Walter Johnson) 103
fudge roll, w/caramel and peanuts (Williamson Salted Nut Roll) 125
gum drops, see "jellied candy," page 91
hard candy:
all flavors (Bonomo Sour Balls) 110
all flavors, except coffee (Charms—in rolls) 113
all flavors, except mint (Life Savers) 111
all flavors (Reed's) 110
butterscotch (Welch's Skimmers) 91
cherry, wild (Welch's Old Fashioned Drops) 87
coffee (Charms—in rolls) 120
honey and horehound (Welch's Old Fashioned Drops) 87
mint, all flavors (Life Savers) 108
rock candy (Dryden & Palmer) 116
root beer (Welch's Drops) 88
jellied candy:
all flavors (Dots) 100
all flavors (Jujubes) 50
all flavors (Jujyfruits) 94
cherry, wild (Mason) 100
lemon, sour (Mason) 100
licorice (Black Crows) 100
licorice (Diamond) 94
orange (Quaker City Slices) 94
raspberry (Red Hot Dollars) 94
root beer (Mason Kegs) 100
spearmint (Quaker City Leaves) 94
spice (Mason Berries) 100
spice (Quaker City Drops) 94
lemon drops, see "hard candy," above, and "jellied candy," above

licorice:
- (Black Crows) 100
- (Diamond Drops) 94
- (Heide Pastilles) 96
- (Switzer) 101
- candy coated (Good and Plenty) 99
- cherry (Switzer Cherry Red) 101

malted milk balls (Walter Johnson) 131

(Mars) 127

marshmallows:
- white (Campfire) 100
- white (Curtiss) 96
- white (Kraft Jet Puff) 94
- white, chocolate covered (Kraft Jet Puff) 127
- chocolate (Kraft) 95
- chocolate, chocolate covered (Kraft) 122
- flavored (Kraft Jet Puff) 94
- macaroon (Kraft) 109

(Milky Way) 120

mint drops, see "hard candy," page 91

mints, afterdinner:
- butter (Kraft) 106
- butter (Richardson) 109
- butter, colored (Kraft Party) 106
- colored (Richardson Pastel) 109
- jelly center (Richardson) 104
- midget (Richardson) 109
- striped (Richardson) 109

mints, chocolate covered:
- (Mason) 200
- (Nestlé's Peppermint Cream) 120
- (Welch's Patties) 108
- (Welch's Peppermint Patties) 108
- (Welch's Thin) 108

nougat, honey flavored, w/nut slivers (Bit-O-Honey) 116

nougat, peanut butter flavored (Bit-O-Peanut Butter) 120

nougat and nuts, chocolate covered:
- (Baby Ruth) 137
- (Oh Henry) 130
- (Powerhouse) 120

nut brittle:
- cashew (Planters Cashew Crunch) 135

peanut (Bonomo) 115
peanut (Kraft) 122
peanut (Planters Peanut Block) 140
peanut, chocolate covered (Kraft) 132

nuts, chocolate covered:
almonds (Kraft) 156
almonds, candy coated (Hershey's) 142
Brazil (Kraft) 164
peanuts (Kraft) 150
peanuts (Welch's) 159
peanuts, candy coated (Hershey's) 139

nuts and caramel, chocolate covered:
almond cluster (Kraft) 156
cashew cluster (Kraft) 152
peanut cluster (Kraft) 151
peanut cluster (Old Nick) 134
peanut cluster (Welch's Royal Cluster) 124
peanut roll, butterscotch flavored (Laddie Bar) 132
peanut roll, chocolate flavored (Choc-O-Nuts) 132

orange drops, see "hard candy," page 91 and "jellied candy," page 91
peanut brittle, see "nut brittle," above
peanut butter, chocolate covered (Reese's Peanut Butter Cups) 148

popcorn and puffs, caramel coated:
corn puffs, w/nuts (Wise Pixies) 103
popcorn (King Korn) 117
popcorn (Wise) 92
popcorn, w/nuts (Cracker Jack) 132
popcorn, w/nuts (Wise) 104

raisins, chocolate covered (Kraft) 118
raisins, chocolate covered (Welch's) 100
rock candy, see "hard candy," page 91
root beer drops, see "hard candy," page 91, and "jellied candy," page 91
(Slo-Poke Sucker) 101
(Snicker) 130
sour balls, see "hard candy," page 91
spice drops, see "jellied candy," page 91
(Sugar Mama) 121
taffy, molasses (Williamson Kisses) 125

taffy, Turkish:
all flavors, except chocolate (Bonomo) 104
chocolate (Bonomo) 109

toffee:
  almond, chocolate covered (Kraft) 142
  chocolate (Kraft) 111
  coffee (Kraft) 112
  rum butter (Kraft) 112
  vanilla (Kraft) 112
(Tootsie Pops and Tootsie Twos) 150
(Tootsie Roll) 115
(Triple Decker) 148

ICE CREAM & FROZEN CONFECTIONS, ½ pint*, except as noted

See also page 166

	CALORIES
frozen custard, chocolate (Tastee-Freez)	320
frozen custard, vanilla (Tastee-Freez)	310
frozen dessert, non-dairy (Sealtest)	270
ice, orange (Sealtest)	266
ice bar, all flavors (Popsicle), 3 fluid oz. bar	70
ice bar, all flavors (Kool Pops), 1 bar, as packaged	27
ice cream:	
all flavors, mix, prepared** (Junket Freezing Mix)	234
chocolate† (Borden's)	258
chocolate, 10% fat (Carnation)	254
chocolate, 10% fat (Meadow Gold)	257
chocolate, 10.8% fat (Sealtest)	287
chocolate, 16.1% fat (Prestige French)	375
chocolate chip, 10% fat (Carnation)	254
strawberry† (Borden's)	253
strawberry, 8.3% fat (Sealtest)	261
strawberry, 10% fat (Carnation)	254
strawberry, 10% fat (Meadow Gold)	252
vanilla† (Borden's)	263
vanilla† (Lady Borden)	350
vanilla, 10% fat (Carnation)	261
vanilla, 10% fat (Meadow Gold)	252
vanilla, 10.2% fat (Sealtest)	264
vanilla, 12.1% fat (Sealtest)	279
vanilla, 16.1% fat (Prestige French)	371
vanilla-chocolate† (Sealtest Checkerboard)	272
vanilla fudge† (Sealtest Royale)	275

ice cream, non-dairy, all flavors (Meadow Gold) 252
ice cream bars:
  vanilla, chocolate coated (Eskimo Pie), 1 bar, as packaged 199
  vanilla, chocolate coated (Eskimo Pie, Jr.), 1 bar, as packaged 114
  vanilla, chocolate coated (Sealtest), 1 bar, as packaged 162
  vanilla, sherbet coated (Creamsicle), 3 fluid oz. bar 96
ice cream patty, mint flavored, chocolate coated (Eskimo Pie
  Thin Mint), 1 patty, as packaged 127
ice cream sandwich (Sealtest), 1 sandwich, as packaged 208
ice cream sandwich, vanilla, chocolate coated (Eskimo),
  1 sandwich, as packaged 124
ice milk:
  vanilla, 3% fat (Borden's) 227
  vanilla, 3% fat (Sealtest) 203
  vanilla, 4% fat (Meadow Gold) 190
  vanilla, 6.25% fat (Lady Borden) 247
ice milk, non-dairy, all flavors (Meadow Gold) 212
ice milk bar, chocolate coated (Sealtest), 1 bar, as packaged 144
ice milk bar, sherbet coated (Eskimo Rainbow Bar), 1 bar, as packaged 68
ice milk patty, vanilla, chocolate coated (Eskimo Do-Nut),
  1 patty, as packaged 115
sherbet:
  all flavors (Meadow Gold) 240
  all flavors, mix, prepared** (Junket Sherbet Mix) 220
  orange (Borden's) 218
  orange (Carnation) 240
  orange (Sealtest) 228
sherbet bar, chocolate (Eskimo Chocolate Fudge), 1 bar, as packaged ... 97
sherbet bar, chocolate (Fudgsicle), 2½ fluid oz. bar 110

** 1 cup*
*** According to package directions*
† Information on fat content unavailable

ICE CREAM CONES & CUPS, 1 piece, as packaged

CALORIES

cone, plain (Comet) 19
cone, colored (Comet) 19
cone, rolled sugar (Comet) 37
cup, plain (Comet) 20
cup, colored (Comet) 20

CHEWING GUM, 1 piece, as packaged, except as noted

	CALORIES
(Adams Sour)	10
(Beech Nut)	10
(Beeman's Pepsin)	9
(Black Jack)	9
(Chiclets)	6
(Chiclets—tiny size), 1 pkg.	65
(Clorets)	6
(Clove)	9
(Dentyne)	5
(Doublemint)	8
(Juicy Fruit)	8
(P.K.)	6
(Wrigley's Spearmint)	8

NUTS, CHIPS, PRETZELS AND SIMILAR SNACKS

17

NUTS, 1 ounce

	CALORIES
almonds:	
barbecued (Blue Diamond)	179
blanched, salted (Blue Diamond)	176
blanched, slivered (Blue Diamond)	176
cheese flavored (Blue Diamond)	179
cocktail, smoke-flavored (Blue Diamond Smokehouse)	179
diced (Blue Diamond)	176
dry roasted (Planters)	180
dry toasted (Franklin)	154
French fried (Blue Diamond)	179
onion-garlic flavored (Blue Diamond)	179
cashews:	
dry roasted (Planters)	180
dry roasted (Skippy)	175
dry toasted (Franklin)	144
oil roasted (Planters)	180
oil roasted (Skippy)	180
filberts, dry toasted (Franklin)	163
mixed:	
dry roasted (Planters)	175
w/peanuts, dry toasted (Franklin Party Mix)	159
wo/peanuts, dry toasted (Franklin Party Mix)	161
w/peanuts, oil roasted (Planters)	185
wo/peanuts, oil roasted (Planters)	180
peanut crisps, dry roasted (Planters)	150
peanuts:	
dry roasted (Lay's)	179
dry roasted (Planters)	170
dry roasted (Skippy)	175

peanuts, continued

dry toasted (Franklin)	154
oil roasted, canned (Planters Cocktail)	185
oil roasted, in bags (Planters Cocktail)	173
oil roasted (Skippy)	180
Spanish, dry roasted (Planters)	175
Spanish, oil roasted (Nabisco)	182
Spanish, oil roasted (Planters)	180
pecans, dry roasted (Planters)	205
walnuts, English (Diamond)	185
walnuts, English (Diamond), chopped, 1 tbsp.	49
pistachios, dry toasted (Franklin)	153

POPCORN & PRETZELS

	CALORIES
popcorn, canned, popped, without butter:	
(Jiffy Pop), 1 cup, loose packed	31
(Jolly Time), 1 cup, loose packed	31
(Pops-Rite), 1 cup, loose packed	39
(Presto-Pop), 1 cup, loose packed	39
(3-Minute), 1 cup, loose packed	38
popcorn, in bags, ready-to-eat:	
butter flavored (Wise), 1 cup, loose packed	42
butter flavored (Wonder), 1 cup, loose packed	45
caramel coated, see "Candy," page 93	
cheese flavored (King Korn), 1 cup, loose packed	40
cheese flavored (Wise), 1 cup, loose packed	50
seasoned (King Korn), 1 cup, loose packed	40
pretzel logs (Bachman), 1 piece, as packaged	18
pretzel nuggets (Bachman Nutzels), 1 piece, as packaged	7
pretzel nuggets (Old London Pretz-L-Nuggets), 1 piece, as packaged	4
pretzel rods (Bachman), 1 piece, as packaged	50
pretzel sticks (Bachman), 1 piece, as packaged	3
pretzel sticks (Nabisco Veri-Thin), 1 piece, as packaged	1
pretzels, 1 piece, as packaged:	
(Bachman B's)	8
(Bachman Beers)	56
(Bachman Medium)	20
(Bachman Teeny)	11
(Bachman Thin)	18

(Nabisco Mister Salty Dutch)	51
(Nabisco Mister Salty 3-Ring)	12
(Nabisco Mister Salty Veri-Thin)	20
(Nabisco Pretzelettes)	6
(Sunshine Extra Thin)	20
w/onion-spice coating (Old London Chick A Dees)	5

CHIPS, PUFFS, RINDS & STICKS, 1 ounce

See also page 148

	CALORIES
(Bows)	162
(Bugles)	162
(Buttons)	146
chips (Nabisco Sip 'N Chips)	145
chips, clam flavored (Snow's Clam Crisps)	166
chips, corn:	
(Fritos)	166
(Old London)	150
(Old London Dipsy Doodles)	150
(Wise)	168
(Wonder)	167
barbecue flavored (Old London Bar-B-Q Doodles)	150
barbecue flavored (Wise)	162
chips, onion flavored (Snow's Onion Crisps)	143
chips, potato:	
(Frito-Lay Ruffles)	156
(Lay's)	156
(Wise)	162
(Wise Ridgies)	162
barbecue flavored (Lay's)	156
barbecue flavored (Wise)	162
onion-garlic flavored (Wise)	162
chips, tortilla (Frito-Lay Doritos)	149
chips, tortilla (Old London)	122
(Daisy*s)	136
puffs, cheese flavored or coated:	
(Frito-Lay Chee • Tos)	159
(Jax Cheese Twists)	138
(Nabisco Flings)	169
(Nabisco Swiss 'n Ham Flings)	148
(Nabisco Shapies)	151

PEANUT BUTTER, DIPS AND MISCELLANEOUS APPETIZERS 18

PEANUT BUTTER, 1 tablespoon

See also page 163

	CALORIES
(Big Top)	72
(Jif)	72
(Peter Pan)	100
(Planters)	100
(Skippy, Chunk)	100
(Skippy, Creamy)	100

DIPS, READY-TO-EAT 8-ounce tin, except as noted

See also "Dip Mixes, Unprepared" and page 147

	CALORIES
bacon and horseradish (Kraft Ready Dip)	568
blue cheese (Kraft Ready Dip)	552
clam (Kraft Ready Dip)	528
dill pickle (Kraft Ready Dip)	536
Jalapeno bean (Fritos), 10½-oz. can	378
Jalapeno bean (Gebhardt)	240
onion soup (Kraft Ready Dip)	544

DIP MIXES, UNPREPARED, 1 ounce

See also "Dips, Ready-to-Eat"

To figure out the caloric content of a prepared dip mix, start by determining the calories in the amount of dry mix you're using, then add the calories in all other ingredients. For example, add about 454 calories if you use a cup of sour cream; about 240 calories if you use a cup of creamed cottage cheese; about 98 calories if you use an ounce of cream cheese. When the dip is prepared, take careful note of its volume (2 cups, 1½ cups, etc.) and you'll be able to determine the calories in an individual serving.

	CALORIES
bacon-onion (Fritos)	106
barbecue (Salada)	119
bleu cheese (Fritos)	117
bleu cheese (Lawry's)	106
Caesar (Fritos)	119
Caesar (Lawry's)	94
cheddar cheese and sesame (Salada)	42
chili con queso (Fritos)	120
dill, kosher (Fritos)	89
dill and chive (Salada)	131
garlic and onion (McCormick)	126
horseradish (Fritos)	105
horseradish (Lawry's)	85
horseradish, w/imitation bacon bits (McCormick)	122
onion (Fritos)	87
onion, French (Salada)	123
onion, green (Fritos)	105
onion, green (Lawry's)	101
onion, toasted (Lawry's)	82
onion, toasted (McCormick)	131
onion and garlic (Salada)	100
taco (Fritos)	105

MISCELLANEOUS SNACKS & APPETIZERS

See also pages 145-146

	CALORIES
beans, green, pickled (Dilly Beans)	56
cheese straws, frozen (Durkee), 1 piece*	29
eel, smoked (Vita), 4 oz.	185
franks "in blankets," frozen (Durkee), 1 piece*	45
gefilte fish, cocktail, in jars (Rokeach Trumps), 1 piece*	8
herring, in sour cream, in jars (Vita), 2 oz.	121
herring, pickled, in jars (Vita), 2 oz.	51

hors d'oeuvres, mixed, frozen (Gretchen Grant), 1 piece* 55
meatballs, cocktail, canned (Cresca), 1 piece* 10
oysters, Japanese, smoked, canned (Cresca), 3½-oz. tin 222
pâté, w/herbs, canned (Le Parfait), 1 oz. 73
pâté, w/truffles, canned (Le Parfait), 1 oz. 73
puffs, beef, frozen (Durkee), 1 piece* 47
puffs, cheese, frozen (Durkee), 1 piece* 59
sausage:
- beef (Cow-Boy Jo's), 1 piece* 81
- beef (Cow-Boy Jo's Beef Jerky), 1 piece* 24
- beef, smoked (Cow-Boy Jo's Smok-O-Roni), 1 piece* 42
- cocktail (Cresca), 4-oz. tin 286
- cocktail (Plumrose), 4-oz. jar 350
- pickled, hot (Lowrey's Freshies), 1 piece* 110
- pickled, Polish (Lowrey's Freshies), 1 piece* 50

shrimp, tiny cocktail (Icy Point), 4½-oz.** can 148
shrimp, tiny cocktail (Pillar Rock),** 4½-oz. can 148
shrimp, tiny cocktail (Snow Mist), 4½-oz.** can 148

* *As packaged*
** *Drained weight of shrimp*

SOFT DRINKS, COCOA, COFFEE AND TEA

19

SOFT DRINKS, 8-ounce glass

See also "Fruit & Fruit Flavored Drinks" and page 168

	CALORIES
bitter lemon (Canada Dry)	104
bitter lemon (Schweppes)	128
bitter orange (Schweppes)	124
cherry soda (Crush)	121
cherry soda (Fanta)	117
club soda (all brands)	trace
cola (Coca-Cola)	96
cola (Pepsi-Cola)	104
cola (Royal Crown)	109
cream soda (Fanta)	130
(Dr. Pepper)	96
fruit, all flavors, mix, prepared* (Kool-Aid)	93
fruit, all flavors, mix, prepared* (Wyler's)	88
ginger ale (Canada Dry)	85
ginger ale (Fanta)	85
ginger ale (Schweppes)	88
ginger beer (Schweppes)	96
grape soda (Crush)	126
grape soda (Fanta)	127
grapefruit soda (Fanta)	115
(Mountain Dew)	116
orange soda (Crush)	117
orange soda (Fanta)	126
quinine water (Canada Dry)	95
quinine water (Fanta)	84
quinine water (Schweppes)	88
root beer (Dad's)	105
root beer (Fanta)	122

root beer (Hire's)	96
(Seven-Up)	97
(Sprite)	96
(Squirt)	91
strawberry soda (Crush)	121
strawberry soda (Fanta)	121
(Wink)	119

* *According to package directions*

COCOA & CHOCOLATE FLAVORED MIXES, DRY, 1 ounce*

See also "Milk Beverages, Flavored"

	CALORIES
chocolate flavored instant mixes:	
(Borden's Double Malted)	116
(Borden's Dutch)	116
(Borden's Hemo)	113
(Flick)	111
(Hershey's)	116
(Nestlé's Quik)	99
cocoa:	
(Hershey's)	111
(Nestlé's Deluxe)	86
instant (Hershey's)	105
instant (Hershey's Sweet Milk)	116
instant (Royal)	110

* *Approximately 3 heaping teaspoons*

COFFEE & TEA, 6-ounce cup or glass, except as noted

	CALORIES
coffee:	
prepared* (Chase & Sanborn)	trace
prepared* (Maxwell House)	2
prepared* (Sanka)	2
prepared* (Yuban)	2
instant, prepared* (Chase & Sanborn)	trace
instant, prepared* (Decaf)	4
instant, prepared* (Kava)	3
instant, prepared* (Maxwell House)	3
instant prepared* (Nescafé)	4

coffee, continued

instant, prepared* (Sanka) 3
instant, prepared* (Yuban) 3

tea:

prepared* (Lipton) 1
prepared* (Tender Leaf) 1
prepared* (Tetley) 3
instant, prepared* (Nestea) .... trace
instant, prepared* (Tender Leaf) 1
iced, mix, presweetened (Nestea), ⅓ pkg. 58
iced, mix, presweetened (Tender Leaf), 1 pkg. 60
punch, fruit flavored (Tender Leaf Fruit 'N Tea Punch), 1 pkg. 100

**According to package directions*

SPIRITS, WINES, LIQUEURS AND RELATED DRINKS 20

DISTILLED SPIRITS*, 1 fluid ounce

Unlike other products in this book, distilled spirits are not listed by brand name. The reason for this is simple: the caloric content in any distilled spirit is determined entirely by the amount of alcohol it contains. The higher the proof (alcoholic content), the more calories in the spirit. Different brands of the same liquor may not taste the same, but if they are the same proof, there is no difference in their caloric content. (*Note:* Remember, this rule applies only to distilled spirits. The calories in other kinds of alcoholic beverages—wines, cordials, etc.—are likely to vary by brand, depending on proof *and* sugar content.) You can cut down on your intake of liquor calories (without cutting down on liquor) by switching to lower proof spirits: for example, by switching from 90-proof gin to 80-proof gin—or 80-proof whatever spirit you prefer. If you normally have two 2-ounce drinks before dinner, the switch from 90-proof to 80-proof liquor will result in a savings of more than 220 calories a week!

	CALORIES
80 proof	67
84 proof	70
86 proof	72
86.8 proof	72
90 proof	75
90.4 proof	75
94 proof	78
94.6 proof	79
97 proof	81
100 proof	83
104 proof	87

distilled spirits, continued

151 proof	126

* *Bourbon; brandy; gin; rum; tequila; vodka; blended, Canadian, Irish, and rye whiskey; Scotch whiskey*

COCKTAILS, BOTTLED, ALCOHOLIC, 1 fluid ounce

	CALORIES
daiquiri (Calvert), 60 proof	63
mai tai (Lemon Hart), 48 proof	60
Manhattan (Calvert), 60 proof	54
Margarita (Calvert), 55 proof	59
martini, gin (Calvert Martini), 70 proof	59
martini, vodka (Calvert Vodka Martini), 75 proof	63
screwdriver, vodka (Old Mr. Boston), 25 proof	39
sour, gin (Calvert), 60 proof	65
sour, tequila (Calvert), 55 proof	61
sour, whiskey (Calvert), 60 proof	65
Tom Collins (Calvert), 60 proof	65

COCKTAIL MIXES, NONALCOHOLIC, 1 fluid ounce, except as noted

When using a nonalcoholic cocktail mix, be sure to "charge" yourself for the liquor you add to the mix (see pages 107-108).

	CALORIES
Bloody Mary (Party Tyme)	29
daiquiri (Holland House)	46
daiquiri (Party Tyme)	35
daiquiri, instant (Party Tyme), 1 premeasured packet	56
gimlet (Holland House)	24
gimlet (Party Tyme)	34
gimlet, instant (Party Tyme), 1 premeasured packet	41
mai tai (Holland House)	26
mai tai (Party Tyme)	19
mai tai, instant (Party Tyme), 1 premeasured packet	53
Manhattan (Holland House)	22
Manhattan (Party Tyme)	23
Margarita (Party Tyme)	22
Margarita, instant (Party Tyme), 1 premeasured packet	38
martini (Party Tyme)	16
martini, dry (Holland House)	10

old-fashioned (Holland House) 9
old-fashioned (Party Tyme) 28
planter's punch (Party Tyme) 37
screwdriver (Party Tyme) 21
sidecar (Holland House) 17
sour, whiskey (Holland House) 50
sour, whiskey (Party Tyme) 29
sour, whiskey, instant (Party Tyme), 1 premeasured packet 54
Tom Collins (Holland House) 58
Tom Collins (Party Tyme) 43
Tom Collins, instant (Party Tyme), 1 premeasured packet 59

TABLE WINES, 4-ounce glass

See also "Aperitif & Dessert Wines"

Bordeaux, red: CALORIES
  (Château La Garde) 108
  (Château Olivier) 108
  (Château Pontet-Canet, Cruse & Fils Frères) 96
  Bordeaux Rouge (Chanson Père & Fils) 108
  Bordeaux Rouge (Cruse & Fils Frères) 84
  Margaux (B & G) 84
  Medoc (Cruse & Fils Frères) 96
  St. Emilion (B & G) 84
  St. Emilion (Cruse & Fils Frères) 92
  St. Julien (Cruse & Fils Frères) 92
Bordeaux, white, Graves (Château Olivier) 108
Bordeaux, white, Graves (Cruse & Fils Frères) 92
Burgundy, red:
  domestic (Gold Seal Vineyards) 109
  domestic (Italian Swiss Colony) 86
  domestic (Taylor Wine Co.) 96
  imported, Beaujolais (Cruse & Fils Frères) 96
  imported, Beaune (Chanson Père & Fils St. Vincent) 108
  imported, Gevrey-Chambertin (Cruse & Fils Frères) 96
  imported, Nuits St. George (B & G) 92
  imported, Pommard (Chanson Père & Fils St. Vincent) 108
  imported, Pommard (Cruse & Fils Frères) 96
Burgundy, sparkling, domestic (Gold Seal Vineyards) 116
Burgundy, sparkling, domestic (Taylor Wine Co.) 104
Catawba (Gold Seal Vineyards) 167
Chablis, domestic (Gold Seal Vineyards) 108

Chablis, domestic (Italian Swiss Colony) 86
Chablis, imported (Chanson Père & Fils St. Vincent) 108
Chablis, imported (Cruse & Fils Frères) 88
Champagne:
domestic (Charles Fournier New York State Brut) 110
domestic (Gold Seal New York State Brut) 113
domestic (Korbel California Brut) 104
domestic (Lejon) 94
domestic (Taylor's Dry Royal Quality New York State) 104
domestic (Taylor's New York State Brut) 100
imported (Bollinger Extra Dry) 114
imported (Mumm's Cordon Rouge Brut) 88
imported (Mumm's Extra Dry) 108
imported (Veuve Clicquot Brut) 104
Champagne, pink, domestic (Gold Seal New York State Extra Dry) 116
Champagne, pink, domestic (Taylor's New York State) 108
Châteauneuf du Pape (B & G) 92
Châteauneuf du Pape (Cruse & Fils Frères) 96
Chianti, domestic (Italian Swiss Colony Tipo) 86
Chianti, imported (Brolio Classico) 88
Chianti, imported (Gancia Classico) 100
claret (Gold Seal Vineyards) 109
claret (Italian Swiss Colony) 86
claret (Taylor Wine Co.) 96
claret-type (Taylor Wine Co. Lake Country Red) 108
concord (Gold Seal Vineyards) 167
Delaware (Gold Seal Vineyards) 116
(Fournier Nature) 109
Kosher, all dry varieties (Manischewitz) 91
Kosher, all medium varieties (Manischewitz) 112
Kosher, all sweet varieties (Manischewitz) 170
Kosher, concord (Mogen David) 200
Liebfraumilch (Anheuser & Fehrs) 84
Liebfraumilch (Dienhard & Co.) 96
Moselle, Bernkasteler (Dienhard & Co.) 92
(Pink Carousel) 167
Pouilly Fuissé (Cruse & Fils Frères) 96
Pouilly Fumé (B & G) 80
(Red Carousel) 139
Rhine, domestic (Gold Seal Vineyards) 108
Rhine, domestic (Italian Swiss Colony) 86
Rhine, domestic (Taylor Wine Co.) 92
rosé, domestic (Italian Swiss Colony) 86

rosé, domestic (Taylor Wine Co.) 92
rosé, imported (Cruse & Fils Frères Vin Rosé) 96
Sancerre (B & G) 80
Sauterne (Gold Seal Vineyards) 116
Sauterne, dry (Gold Seal Vineyards) 108
Sauterne, dry (Taylor Wine Co.) 108
(White Carousel) 167
Zinfandel (Italian Swiss Colony) 86

APERITIF & DESSERT WINES, 4-ounce glass

See also "Table Wines"

CALORIES

Asti Spumante (Gancia) 168
(Dubonnet Blonde) 151
(Dubonnet Red) 190
Madeira (Leacock) 160
Madeira (Sandeman & Co.) 168
Muscatel (Gold Seal Vineyards) 210
Port:
  all varieties, domestic (Gold Seal Vineyards) 210
  ruby, domestic (Italian Swiss Colony Gold Medal) 171
  ruby, domestic (Taylor Wine Co.) 200
  tawny, domestic (Taylor Wine Co.) 192
  ruby, imported (Robertson Bros. & Co. Black Label) 184
  ruby, imported (Sandeman & Co.) 184
  ruby, imported (Sandeman & Co. Partners') 188
  tawny, imported (Sandeman & Co.) 184
Sauternes (B & G) 128
Sauternes (Chateau Voigny) 128
sherry:
  domestic (Gold Seal Private Reserve New York State) 185
  domestic (Taylor's New York State) 176
  domestic (Taylor's New York State Cream) 200
  imported (Williams & Humbert Dry Sack) 160
sherry, dry:
  domestic (Gold Seal Private Reserve New York State Cocktail) 162
  domestic (Taylor's New York State Pale Dry Cocktail) 152
  imported (Sandeman Cocktail) 144
vermouth, dry:
  domestic (Lejon Extra Dry) 136
  domestic (Taylor's Extra Dry) 136

vermouth, dry, continued
imported (C & P Extra Dry) 148
imported (Gancia Dry) 168
imported (Noilly Prat Extra Dry) 136
vermouth, sweet:
domestic (Lejon) 175
domestic (Taylor Wine Co.) 176
imported (Noilly Prat) 172
imported (C & P) 188
imported (Gancia Bianco) 176
imported (Gancia Rosso) 204
white tokay (Taylor Wine Co.) 192

CORDIALS & LIQUEURS, 1 fluid ounce

See also "Fruit Brandies" and "Flavored Gins and Vodkas"

CALORIES
anise-licorice (DuBouchett Absant), 100 proof 84
anise-licorice (Pernod), 90 proof 79
anisette:
all colors (Bols), 56 proof 111
all colors (DuBouchett), 60 proof 85
white (Dolfi), 50 proof 102
white (DuBouchett), 48 proof 75
white (Garnier), 54 proof 82
white (Old Mr. Boston), 60 proof 90
white (Old Mr. Boston Connoisseur), 42 proof 64
apricot (Bols), 60 proof 96
apricot (Dolfi), 70 proof 100
apricot (DuBouchett), 48 proof 63
(B & B), 86 proof 94
(Benai), 86 proof 110
(Benai & Brandy), 85 proof 89
(Benedictine), 86 proof 112
blackberry (Bols), 60 proof 96
blackberry (Dolfi), 70 proof 93
blackberry (DuBouchett), 48 proof 70
bourbon, peach flavored (Old Mr. Boston), 70 proof 100
brandy, see "Distilled Spirits," pages 107-108
brandy, flavored:
apricot (Bols), 70 proof 100
apricot (DuBouchett), 70 proof 81

apricot (Garnier), 70 proof 86
apricot (Old Mr. Boston), 70 proof 100
apricot (Old Mr. Boston Connoisseur Apricot & Brandy), 42 proof 75
blackberry (Bols), 70 proof 100
blackberry (DuBouchett), 70 proof 88
blackberry (Garnier), 70 proof 86
blackberry (Leroux), 70 proof 94
blackberry (Old Mr. Boston), 70 proof 100
blackberry (Old Mr. Boston Connoisseur Blackberry & Brandy), 42 proof 75
cherry (Bols), 70 proof 100
cherry (DuBouchett), 70 proof 88
cherry (Garnier), 70 proof 86
cherry, wild (Old Mr. Boston), 70 proof 100
coffee (DuBouchett), 70 proof 88
coffee (Old Mr. Boston), 70 proof 74
ginger (DuBouchett), 70 proof 75
ginger (Garnier), 70 proof 74
ginger (Old Mr. Boston), 70 proof 74
ginger (Old Mr. Boston Connoisseur Ginger & Brandy), 42 proof 75
peach (Bols), 70 proof 100
peach (DuBouchett), 70 proof 88
peach (Garnier), 70 proof 86
peach (Old Mr. Boston), 70 proof 100
peach (Old Mr. Boston Connoisseur Peach & Brandy), 42 proof 75

(Brighton Punch), 91 proof 89
cherry (Bols), 60 proof 96
cherry (Dolfi), 64 proof 87
cherry (DuBouchett), 48 proof 72
cherry, Danish (Cherry Heering), 49 proof 80
chocolate, mint (Vandermint), 60 proof 90
coffee (Coffee Southern), 55 proof 85
coffee, Jamaican (Tia Maria), 63 proof 92
coffee, Turkish (Pasha), 53 proof 100
crèmes:
de almond (DuBouchett), 60 proof 101
de almond (Garnier Crème d'Amande), 60 proof 111
de apricot (Old Mr. Boston Connoisseur), 42 proof 66
de banana (Dolfi Crème de Banane), 50 proof 100
de banana (Garnier Crème de Banane), 60 proof 96
de banana (Old Mr. Boston Connoisseur), 42 proof 66
de black cherry (Old Mr. Boston Connoisseur), 42 proof 66
de blackberry (Old Mr. Boston Connoisseur), 42 proof 66
de cacao, all colors (Bols), 54 proof 101

crèmes, continued

de cacao, all colors (Dolfi), 50 proof 100
de cacao, all colors (DuBouchett), 48 proof 101
de cacao, all colors (DuBouchett), 54 proof 106
de cacao, all colors (Garnier), 54 proof 97
de cacao, all colors (Old Mr. Boston), 54 proof 95
de cacao, all colors (Old Mr. Boston Connoisseur), 42 proof 84
de cacao, brown (Leroux), 54 proof 100
de cacao, white (Leroux), 54 proof 94
de cassis (Dolfi), 36 proof 97
de cassis (DuBouchett), 35 proof 79
de cassis (Garnier), 36 proof 83
de coffee (Old Mr. Boston Connoisseur), 42 proof 66
de menthe, all colors (Bols), 60 proof 112
de menthe, all colors (DuBouchett), 46 proof 95
de menthe, all colors (DuBouchett), 60 proof 101
de menthe, all colors (Garnier), 60 proof 110
de menthe, all colors (Old Mr. Boston), 60 proof 94
de menthe, all colors (Old Mr. Boston Connoisseur), 42 proof 66
de menthe, green (Dolfi), 54 proof 103
de menthe, green (Leroux), 60 proof 110
de menthe, white (Dolfi), 54 proof 104
de menthe, white (Leroux), 60 proof 104
de noisette (Dolfi), 54 proof 91
de noyaux (Bols), 60 proof 115
de peach (Old Mr. Boston Connoisseur), 42 proof 66

curaçao:

blue (Bols), 64 proof 105
orange (Bols), 64 proof 100
orange (Dolfi), 80 proof 107
orange (DuBouchett), 60 proof 86
orange (Garnier), 60 proof 100
orange (Leroux), 60 proof 87

(Drambuie), 80 proof 110
(Goldwasser), 80 proof 104
(Honey Punch), 70 proof 80
kümmel (DuBouchett), 48 proof 65
kümmel (DuBouchett), 70 proof 83
kümmel (Garnier), 70 proof 75
kümmel (Old Mr. Boston), 70 proof 78
maraschino (DuBouchett), 60 proof 85
maraschino (Garnier), 60 proof 94
peach (Bols), 60 proof 96

peach (Dolfi), 70 proof 103
peach (DuBouchett), 48 proof 67
peppermint schnapps:
  (DuBouchett), 48 proof 70
  (DuBouchett), 60 proof 85
  (Garnier), 60 proof 83
  (Old Mr. Boston), 60 proof 78
  (Old Mr. Boston Connoisseur), 42 proof 60
raspberry (DuBouchett), 50 proof 56
rock & rum (DuBouchett), 50 proof 77
rock & rye:
  (DuBouchett), 60 proof 78
  (DuBouchett), 70 proof 86
  (Garnier), 70 proof 83
  (Old Mr. Boston), 60 proof 94
  (Old Mr. Boston Connoisseur), 48 proof 72
sloe gin:
  (Bols), 66 proof 85
  (Dolfi Prunelle), 80 proof 114
  (DuBouchett), 48 proof 68
  (DuBouchett), 60 proof 71
  (Garnier), 60 proof 83
  (Old Mr. Boston), 70 proof 76
  (Old Mr. Boston Connoisseur), 42 proof 50
(Southern Comfort), 100 proof 120
strawberry, wild (Dolfi Fraise des Bois), 44 proof 88
tangerine (Dolfi), 60 proof 97
triple sec:
  (Bols), 78 proof 113
  (Dolfi), 80 proof 107
  (DuBouchett), 48 proof 61
  (Garnier), 60 proof 83
  (Leroux), 80 proof 105
  (Old Mr. Boston), 60 proof 105
  (Old Mr. Boston Connoisseur), 42 proof 97

FLAVORED GIN & VODKA, 1 fluid ounce

See also "Cordials & Liqueurs"

CALORIES

gin:
  lemon (DuBouchett), 70 proof 59

gin, continued

lemon (Old Mr. Boston), 70 proof	76
mint (DuBouchett), 70 proof	70
mint (Old Mr. Boston), 70 proof	100
orange (DuBouchett), 70 proof	67
orange (Old Mr. Boston), 70 proof	76
vodka:	
cherry, wild (Old Mr. Boston), 70 proof	100
grape (Old Mr. Boston), 70 proof	100
lemon (Old Mr. Boston), 70 proof	100
lime (Old Mr. Boston), 70 proof	100
orange (Old Mr. Boston), 70 proof	100
peppermint (Old Mr. Boston), 70 proof	90

FRUIT BRANDIES, 1 fluid ounce

See also "Cordials & Liqueurs"

	CALORIES
kirsch (Dolfi), 90 proof	78
kirsch (Dolfi Cordon d'Or), 96 proof	83
kirsch (Garnier), 96 proof	83
raspberry (Dolfi Framboise), 90 proof	78
raspberry (Dolfi Cordon d'Or Framboise), 96 proof	83
yellow plum (Dolfi Mirabelle), 90 proof	78
yellow plum (Dolfi Cordon d'Or Mirabelle), 96 proof	83

ALE, BEER & MALT LIQUOR, 8-ounce glass

	CALORIES
ale (Red Cap)	106
beer:	
(Brauhaus)	100
(Budweiser)	105
(Busch Bavarian)	105
(Carling Black Label)	108
(Carlsberg, Light de Luxe)	102
(Carlsberg, Dark "19-B")	160
(Falstaff)	100
(Grand Union)	100
(Heidelberg)	98
(Heidelberg Light Pilsner)	86

(Heileman's Special Export)	106
(Kingsbury)	97
(Michelob)	107
(Old Dutch)	100
(Old Ranger)	100
(Old Style)	104
(Pabst Blue Ribbon)	100
(Pearl)	97
(Pilser's Original)	100
(Rheingold)	110
(Rupert-Knickerbocker)	105
(Schaefer)	106
(Schlitz)	103
(Stag)	101
(Tudor)	100
malt liquor (Champale)	104
malt liquor (Country Club)	115

BEER, NONALCOHOLIC, 8-ounce glass

	CALORIES
(Maltcrest)	47
(Metbrew)	47
(Zing)	43

NEW FOODS & NEW BRANDS: 1700 BONUS LISTINGS! 21

Unlike the first edition of *The Brand-Name Calorie Counter,* this expanded edition carries no listings for so-called basic foods: fresh fruits, vegetables, meat, poultry, etc. What's more, I admit to eliminating that chapter without so much as blushing. Good-bye dandelion greens, mustard spinach, and kohlrabi! Make room for Sara Lee, Betty Crocker, Mrs. Smith, the Green Giant and dozens more!

Let other books list goodies such as roast opossum (meat only, 251 calories), scalded pork stomach (ugh! 172 calories per four ounces), and raw muskellunge (whatever it is, 242 calories a pound). This is an *all* brand-name counter, and there simply isn't room for generic foods. Novice dieters—and those who thrive on pickled tripe—can pick up an excellent generalized counter for only 25¢ (*Count Your Calories;* Dell Purse Books); however, I'm confident that perennial dieters care more about the calories in Good Humors than gooseberries, Pizza Rolls than persimmons.

Let me add quickly that you will, of course, find many hundreds of "basic" foods in *The Brand-Name Calorie Counter.* Neither man nor the food industry can subsist on snacks alone, and though you won't, for example, find raw potatoes in the book, you will find cooked potatoes—boiled, baked and stuffed, candied, creamed, French fried, mashed, whipped, scalloped, and au gratin (not to mention good old potato chips, crisps, and sticks)!

Very simply, there are few foods, basic or otherwise, missing from the book because there are few foods that the amazing American food industry hasn't packaged—and, in my opinion, frequently improved upon. I think I'm a good cook, but I admit freely that my Welsh rarebit doesn't compare to Stouffer's, my chocolate pudding isn't as smooth as Cool 'n Creamy, my vegetable soup seems pallid next to Campbell's new Chunky. And maybe I'm just not imaginative, but it never occurred to me to whip up Parmesan-style zucchini (thank you, Mrs. Paul's) or pork with a sweet and sour sauce (kisses to Chun King)!

All of which brings us back to this expanded section: nearly fifty pages of new foods and/or new brands; the caloric content of another 1700 products! However, this section isn't all that's new by any means. Readers of the original book will find some new listings in "old" categories (for example, Chinese and Mexican foods), but, more important, *there are many changes in the caloric content of "old" foods.*

These changes don't matter, of course, if you're a new reader, but they *do* matter if you've practically memorized the first book. For example, Morton's spaghetti-and-meatball frozen dinner no longer contains 530 calories. The size is the same, but recipe changes have resulted in the caloric content dropping to 364! McCormick's spaghetti sauce has 30 calories less per half cup; a Pepperidge Farm apple turnover has 25 calories more. In short, if you've been using the original *Brand-Name Calorie Counter*—stop now! Recheck the data on your favorite foods to see if there have been changes.

Since publication of the first edition of the book, I've been flooded with mail from dieters and others, asking questions about brand-name foods that unfortunately I couldn't answer. For that reason, I'm delighted to be able to close with a message from the Grocery Manufacturers of America (G.M.A. is a trade association, representing every major food producer in the country; just as the A.M.A. is the voice of the medical profession, G.M.A. is the voice of the food industry). George W. Koch, president of G.M.A., asked that this message reach readers of *The Brand-Name Calorie Counter:*

"Do you need more information about the products in this book? Manufacturers are anxious to let you know about the contents and nutritive value of their products. Since every package states the name and address of its manufacturer, additional information may be obtained by writing."

C.T.N.

BREADS, ROLLS & MUFFINS, 1 piece or slice, as packaged

See also Chapter 1

	CALORIES
biscuit, refrigerator, baked (Pillsbury Buttermilk)	60
biscuit, refrigerator, baked (Pillsbury Flaky Baking Powder)	67
biscuit, refrigerator, baked (Pillsbury Hungry Jack)	103
bread:	
cheese (Pepperidge Farm Party Slices)	18
cinnamon raisin (Wonder)	59
cracked wheat, honey (Wonder)	65
(Profile—dark)	56
(Profile—light)	58
pumpernickel (Pepperidge Farm Party Slices)	20
pumpernickel (Wonder)	54
rye (Pepperidge Farm Party Slices)	13
rye (Pepperidge Farm Seedless)	82
rye (Wonder)	55
rye (Wonder Beefsteak)	82
white (Pepperidge Farm Toasting)	85
white (Pepperidge Farm Very Thin)	39
whole wheat (Wonder)	57
(Wonder Golden Wheat)	65
bread, sweet, canned, ½-inch slice:	
banana nut (Dromedary)	71
chocolate nut (Cross & Blackwell)	65
chocolate nut (Dromedary)	87
date nut (Dromedary)	75
fruit and nut (Crosse & Blackwell)	77
orange nut (Crosse & Blackwell)	76
orange nut (Dromedary)	77
spice nut (Crosse & Blackwell)	63
muffins:	
blueberry, frozen (Morton)	116
cinnamon raisin, frozen (Howard Johnson's Toastees)	105
corn, frozen (Morton)	133
pound cake, frozen (Howard Johnson's Toastees)	105
raisin (Drake's Raisin Snacks—1.08-oz. size)	112
raisin (Drake's Raisin Snacks—2¼-oz. size)	233
raisin (Hostess Raisin Rounds)	164

rolls:
(Pepperidge Farm Butter Crescent) 135
(Pepperidge Farm Old Fashioned Butter) 57
(Pepperidge Farm Party—finger) 75
(Pepperidge Farm Party—round) 45
frankfurter (Pepperidge Farm) 114
frozen (Sara Lee Finger) 53
frozen (Sara Lee Parkerhouse) 52
frozen (Sara Lee Sesame Seed) 52
hamburger (Pepperidge Farm) 112
hamburger or hot dog (Wonder) 124
refrigerator, baked (Pillsbury Butterflake) 60
refrigerator, baked (Pillsbury Crescent) 106
refrigerator, baked (Pillsbury Parkerhouse) 64
refrigerator, baked (Pillsbury Snowflake) 62

CRACKERS, 1 piece, as packaged, except as noted

See also Chapter 1

CALORIES

bacon flavored (Keebler Bacon Toast) 15
cheese flavored (Cheez-Pix) 6
cheese flavored (Keebler Cheese Toast) 16
cheese flavored (Pepperidge Farm Cheddar Goldfish), 10 pieces 28
cheese flavored (Pepperidge Farm Toasted Thins) 12
cracker sandwich, cheese (Huntley & Palmer's) 105
cracker sandwich, cheese-bacon (Nabisco Cheese 'n Bacon) 33
cracker sandwich, malted milk-peanut butter (Nabisco) 37
cracker sandwich, peanut butter-jelly (Nabisco) 30
ham flavored (Nabisco Appeteasers) 3
onion flavored:
(Keebler Onion Toasts) 15
(Manischewitz Onion Tams) 13
(Nabisco Appeteasers) 3
(Pepperidge Farm Goldfish), 10 pieces 28
(Pepperidge Farm Toasted Thins) 12
Parmesan flavored (Pepperidge Farm Goldfish), 10 pieces 28
pizza flavored (Pepperidge Farm Goldfish), 10 pieces 29
pretzel-type (Pepperidge Farm Goldfish), 10 pieces 29
rye:
(Peek Frean's Rye Crispbread) 31

(Pepperidge Farm Toasted Thins) 11
(Ry-Krisp) 21
(Sunshine All-Rye) 20
pizza flavored (Pizza Ry-Krisp) 8
seasoned (Ry-Krisp) 25
saltines, soda and water crackers:
(Huntley & Palmer's Fortts' Oliver) 35
(Jacob's Golden Puffs) 35
(Jacob's Water Biscuits—large) 35
(Keebler Milk Lunch) 27
(Pepperidge Farm Lightly Salted Goldfish), 10 pieces 28
(Waldorf Low-Sodium) 14
(Zesta) 12
sesame (Sunshine Sesamée Bread Wafers) 23
sesame-garlic (Pepperidge Farm Goldfish) 29
toasted (Pepperidge Farm White Toasted Thins) 12
wheat (Jacob's Goldgrain) 35

EGG MIXES, FROZEN BREAKFASTS, FRENCH TOAST & RELATED PRODUCTS

See also Chapter 2

CALORIES

egg omelets:
cheese, mix (McCormick Seasoning Mix), 1 serving* 168
mushroom, mix (McCormick Seasoning Mix), 1 serving* 163
Western, mix Durkee), 1-serving pkg.** 170
Western, mix (McCormick Seasoning Mix), 1 serving* 164
eggs, scrambled:
mix (Durkee), 1-serving pkg.** 124
w/imitation bacon bits, mix (Durkee), 1-serving pkg.** 181
w/sausage and potatoes, frozen (Swanson Breakfast), 5-oz. pkg. 452
French toast:
frozen (Downyflake), 1 slice 138
mix (McCormick Batter Mix), 1 slice** 119
and sausage patties, frozen (Swanson Breakfast), 4½-oz. pkg. 336
pancakes, frozen (Downyflake), 1 cake 72
pancakes and sausage, frozen (Swanson Breakfast), 6½-oz. pkg. 340
waffles, frozen (Downyflake), 1 waffle 55

* *One-egg omelet, prepared according to package directions*
** *Prepared according to package directions*

CHEESE, 1 ounce, except as noted

See also Chapter 5

	CALORIES
American, natural (Kraft)	113
American, grated (Kraft) 1 tbsp.	31
blue (Foremost Blue Moon)	105
blue (Foremost Blue Chip Brand)	99
brick, natural (Borden's)	105
Brie (Dorman's Endeco)	100
Camembert (Kraft Tiny Dane)	85
cheddar (Coon Brand)	113
cheddar (Martin's Rabbit Brand)	113
cheddar, shredded (Kraft Cracker Barrel Brand), 1 tbsp.	34
Colby (Borden's)	111
Colby (Kraft Cracker Barrel Brand)	111
Colby (Jay Brand)	111
cottage, creamed:	
(Breakstone), ½ cup	115
(Breakstone Low Fat), ½ cup	90
(Kraft), ½ cup	107
(Pet), ½ cup	127
w/chive (Breakstone), ½ cup	115
w/chive (Sealtest), ½ cup	106
w/chive-pepper (Sealtest), ½ cup	102
w/peach-pineapple (Sealtest), ½ cup	115
w/pineapple (Breakstone), ½ cup	132
cottage, creamed partially (Foremost So-Lo), ½ cup	94
cottage, creamed partially (Pet), ½ cup	103
cottage, creamed partially (Sealtest Light 'n Lively), ½ cup	77
cottage, uncreamed (Breakstone Pot Style), ½ cup	85
cottage, uncreamed (Breakstone Skim Milk), ½ cup	88
cream cheese:	
(Breakstone)	86
(Kraft Philadelphia Brand)	104
imitation (Borden's Velva Creme)	91
imitation (Kraft Philadelphia Brand)	52
whipped (Temp-Tee)	86
whipped, w/salami (Kraft)	88
whipped, w/smoked salmon (Kraft)	90

Edam (Dorman's Endeco) 105
farmer (Breakstone Midget) 39
fontina (Kraft) 114
Gouda (Jay Brand) 108
Gruyère (Kraft Imported Switzerland Crown Brand) 110
Limburger (Dorman's Endeco) 100
Limburger (Mohawk Valley Brand) 98
Mozzarella (Dorman's Endeco) 85
Mozzarella, shredded (Kraft), 1 tbsp. 26
Neufchâtel, w/olive and pimento (Borden's) 81
Neufchâtel, w/pimento (Borden's) 82
Neufchâtel, w/relish (Borden's) 81
Parmesan, grated (Borden's), 1 tbsp. 30
Parmesan, shredded (Kraft), 1 tbsp. 23
Parmesan-Romano, grated (Kraft) 25
pinconning (Kraft) 113
pizza, shredded (Kraft), 1 tbsp. 29
Port Salut (Dorman's Endeco) 100
Provolone (Dorman's Endeco) 90
Ricotta, moist (Breakstone) 51
Ricotta, moist (Frigo) 39
Ricotta, moist (Kraft) 47
Romano, shredded (Kraft), 1 tbsp. 23
Romano-Parmesan, grated (Kraft), 1 tbsp. 26
Romano-Parmesan, bacon-smoke flavored, grated (Kraft), 1 tbsp. 25
Romano-Parmesan, garlic flavored, grated (Kraft), 1 tbsp. 25
Romano-Parmesan, onion flavored, grated (Kraft), 1 tbsp. 27
Sage (Kraft) 113
tilsiter (Dorman's Endeco) 95

CHEESE FOODS & SPREADS, 1 ounce

See also Chapter 5

CALORIES

cheese foods:
  American (Borden's) 91
  pimento (Borden's) 91
  w/salami (Kraft) 94
  Swiss (Borden's) 91
cheese spreads:
  w/bacon (Kraft Squeez-A-Snak) 83

cheese spreads, continued

blue (Borden's "Vera Blue") 91
w/garlic (Borden's) 82
w/garlic (Kraft Squeez-A-Snak) 84
hickory smoke flavored (Kraft Squeez-A-Snak) 83
w/Jalapeno pepper and pimento (Cheese Whiz Jalapeno Pepper) 76
Limburger (Borden's) 82
onion, French (Snack Mate) 85
pimento (Kraft Squeez-A-Snak) 86
sharp (Kraft Squeez-A-Snak) 85
Swiss (Kraft) 93

YOGURT, 8-ounce cup, except as noted

See also Chapter 4

CALORIES

plain (Breakstone) 144
plain (Pet) 157
plain (Sealtest Light 'n Lively) 146
plain (Yami), 8 oz.* 140
flavored:
all flavors (Dannon "Danny"), 4-fl.-oz. carton 130
all flavors (Meadow Gold Swiss Style), 8 oz.* 245
all flavors (Meadow Gold Western Style), 8 oz.* 249
all flavors (Sanna Swiss Miss), 4-fl.-oz. carton 125
all flavors except vanilla (Yami), 8 oz.* 240
apple, cinnamon (Breakstone) 284
apple, Dutch (Dannon) 260
apple, spiced (Sealtest Light 'n Lively) 282
apricot (Breakstone) 286
blueberry (Breakstone) 284
blueberry (Breakstone Swiss Parfait) 303
blueberry (Sealtest Light 'n Lively) 298
boysenberry (Dannon) 260
cherry (Dannon) 260
cherry, black (Breakstone Swiss Parfait), 5-fl.-oz. carton 186
cherry-vanilla (Borden's Swiss Style) 270
cranberry-orange (Borden's Swiss Style) 270
fruit cup (Dannon) 260
lemon (Sealtest Light 'n Lively) 264
lime (Borden's Swiss Style) 270

orange, Mandarin (Breakstone Swiss Parfait) 303
orange, Mandarin (Breakstone Swiss Parfait), 5-fl.-oz. carton 189
peach (Borden's Swiss Style) 258
peach (Breakstone Swiss Parfait) 290
peach (Sealtest Light 'n Lively) 290
peach Melba (Breakstone Swiss Parfait), 5-fl.-oz. carton 195
pineapple (Breakstone) 286
pineapple (Sealtest Light 'n Lively) 276
prune (Breakstone) 284
prune (Sealtest Light 'n Lively) 296
raspberry (Breakstone) 284
raspberry, red (Breakstone Swiss Parfait) 293
raspberry, red (Sealtest Light 'n Lively) 258
strawberry (Breakstone) 286
strawberry (Breakstone Swiss Parfait) 291
strawberry (Breakstone Swiss Parfait), 5-fl.-oz. carton 181
strawberry (Sealtest Light 'n Lively) 268
vanilla (Breakstone) 208
vanilla (Sealtest Light 'n Lively) 220
vanilla (Yami), 8 oz.* 188
flavored, frozen bars, 2½ fl. oz.:
pineapple-orange, orange coated (Dannon Danny-on-a-Stick) 70
raspberry, red, chocolate coated (Dannon Danny-on-a-Stick) 90
strawberry, chocolate coated (Dannon Danny-on-a-Stick) 90

* *Approximately 7/8 cup*

FRUITS, ½ cup, except as noted

See also Chapter 3

CALORIES

apple fritters, fried, frozen (Mrs. Paul's), 12-oz. pkg. 712
apple rings, spiced, canned (Musselman's), 4 rings* 84
applesauce, sweetened, canned and in jars:
(Hunt's Snack Pack), 5-oz. can 94
(Mott's Country Style with Cinnamon) 105
(Mott's Golden Delicious) 105
(Mott's McIntosh) 105
(Musselman's) 112
(Stokely-Van Camp) 105
apple slices, swt., canned (Musselman's) 112

apricots, swt., canned (Hunt's) 103
apricots, swt., canned (Libby's) 97
apricots, swt., canned (Stokely-Van Camp—whole or halves) 92
blackberries, swt., canned (Musselman's) 107
blueberries, swt., canned (Musselman's) 119
blueberries, swt., frozen (Birds Eye Quick Thaw) 135
blueberries, unswt., frozen (Seabrook Farms) 45
cherries:
  sour, red, canned (Stokely-Van Camp) 52
  sweet, swt., canned (Musselman's) 96
  sweet, dark, swt., canned (Stokely-Van Camp) 88
  sweet, light, swt., canned (Stokely-Van Camp) 88
  sweet, swt., frozen (Birds Eye Quick Thaw) 122
crab apples, swt., canned (Musselman's), 1 apple* 36
fruit cocktail, sweetened, canned:
  (Hunt's) 89
  (Hunt's Snack Pack Fruit Cup), 5-oz. can 106
  (Libby's Fruits 'n Juice) 94
  (Stokely-Van Camp) 88
grapefruit sections*, swt., canned (Stokely-Van Camp) 57
grapefruit sections*, unswt., fresh, dairy-packed (Kraft) 32
orange sections*, unswt., fresh, dairy-packed (Kraft) 30
peaches, sweetened:
  canned (Hunt's Snack Pack), 5-oz. can 106
  canned (Libby's) 118
  canned (Stokely-Van Camp—Cling and Freestone; halves or slices) 88
  frozen (Birds Eye Quick Thaw) 87
  frozen (Seabrook Farms) 106
pears, swt., canned (Hunt's) 90
pears, swt., canned (Libby's) 82
pears, swt., canned (Stokely-Van Camp) 86
pineapple chunks, in extra heavy syrup, swt., canned (Dole) 84
pineapple chunks, in heavy syrup, swt., canned (Stokely-Van Camp) 84
pineapple, crushed, in heavy syrup, swt., canned (Stokely-Van Camp) 100
plums, swt., canned (Musselman's) 103
plums, swt., canned (Stokely-Van Camp) 90
raspberries, black, swt., canned (Musselman's) 109
strawberries, swt., frozen (Birds Eye Quick Thaw) 122
strawberries, unswt., frozen (Seabrook Farms—whole) 42

* *Drained of syrup or liquid*

FRUIT & VEGETABLE JUICES, 6 oz. glass, except as noted

See also Chapters 3 and 7

	CALORIES
apple, bottled or canned (Musselman's)	78
blackcurrant, swt., bottled (Ribena)	83
fig and prune, bottled (Fig 'N Prune)	132
grapefruit:	
fresh, dairy-packed (Kraft)	72
canned (Libby's)	62
canned (Stokely-Van Camp)	61
swt., fresh, dairy-packed (Kraft)	90
swt., canned (Stokely-Van Camp)	78
swt., frozen (Minute Maid)	85
swt., frozen (Snow Crop)	85
lemon, bottled (Rose's), 2 tbsp.	11
orange:	
fresh, dairy-packed (Foremost)	100
fresh, dairy-packed (Kraft)	90
fresh, dairy-packed (Pet)	76
canned (Libby's)	76
dairy-packed (Kraft—from concentrate)	96
frozen, reconstituted* (Libby's)	77
frozen, reconstituted* (Stokely-Van Camp)	90
imitation, frozen, reconstituted* (Orange Plus)	100
orange-grapefruit, fresh, dairy-packed (Kraft)	90
orange-grapefruit, canned (Stokely-Van Camp Citrusip)	68
orange-grapefruit, swt., canned (Stokely-Van Camp Citrusip)	78
orange-pineapple, dairy-packed (Kraft)	96
pineapple, canned (Stokely-Van Camp)	108
prune, w/lemon, bottled or canned (Sunsweet)	128
prune, apricot-apple, bottled (Sunsweet)	95
tomato, bottled or canned (BC)	39
tomato, canned (Libby's), 5½-oz. can	37
tomato, canned (Sacramento)	33
tomato, canned (Stokely-Van Camp)	36
tomato cocktail, bottled or canned (Mott's)	39
tomato-beef broth cocktail, bottled or canned (Beefamato)	73
tomato-clam broth cocktail, bottled or canned (Clamato)	86

* *According to package directions*

FRUIT & FRUIT FLAVORED DRINKS, 8-ounce glass

See also Chapters 3 and 19

	CALORIES
apple-cranberry, bottled or canned (Mott's)	127
apricot nectar, canned (Sunsweet)	105
apricot-apple, canned (BC)	128
berry, wild, canned (Hi-C)	122
cherry-apple, canned (BC)	136
cider, sweet, bottled (Mott's)	112
cider, cherry flavor, bottled, (Mott's)	112
cider, cranberry flavor, bottled (Mott's)	112
citrus, canned (Hi-C Cooler)	122
citrus, imitation, mix, prepared* (Instant Replay)	89
cranberry-grape, bottled (Grapeberry)	163
cranberry-prune, bottled (Cranprune)	164
grape:	
canned (Stokely-Van Camp)	115
dairy-packed (Tropicana)	93
mix, prepared* (Knox Gelatin)	146
mix, prepared* (Salada)	99
imitation, mix, prepared* (Wyler's)	85
grapeade, w/lemon, frozen, reconstituted* (Welchade)	120
grape-apple, canned (BC)	144
grapefruit, dairy-packed (Tropicana)	93
lemon, dairy-packed (Sealtest)	121
lemonade, bottled or canned (Stokely-Van Camp)	113
lemonade, frozen, reconstituted* (Libby's)	90
lemonade, mix, prepared* (Salada)	96
lemon-limeade, frozen, reconstituted* (Minute Maid)	100
lemon-limeade, frozen, reconstituted* (Snow Crop)	100
limeade, frozen, reconstituted * (Snow Crop)	100
limeade, imitation, mix, prepared* (Wyler's)	85
orange:	
canned (Stokely-Van Camp)	114
dairy-packed (Borden's)	109
dairy-packed (Sealtest Deluxe)	113
dairy-packed (Tropicana)	93
mix, prepared* (Salada)	95
imitation, mix, prepared* (Instant Replay)	88

orangeade, frozen, reconstituted* (Snow Crop) 125
orange-apricot, canned (BC) 120
orange-banana, canned (BC) 120
orange-grapefruit, canned (BC) 120
orange-pineapple, canned (BC) 128
pineapple-grapefruit, canned (Stokely-Van Camp Ping) 116
pineapple-grapefruit, dairy-packed (Tropicana) 93
pineapple-orange, canned (Stokely-Van Camp Pong) 111
punch:
  berry, canned (Hawaiian Punch Very Berry) 110
  fruit, canned (Hawaiian Punch Apple Red) 110
  fruit, canned (Mott's Tropical) 120
  fruit, canned (Stokely-Van Camp) 114
  fruit, dairy-packed (Tropicana) 93
  fruit, frozen, reconstituted* (Hawaiian Punch Fruit Juicy Red) 111
  fruit, mix, prepared* (Salada) 100
  fruit, imitation, mix, prepared* (Wyler's) 85
  grape, frozen, reconstituted* (Hawaiian Punch) 110
  lemon-pink, canned (Hawaiian Punch) 110
  pineapple, canned (Hawaiian Punch) 110
raspberry, imitation, mix, prepared* (Wyler's) 85
strawberry, imitation, mix, prepared* (Wyler's) 85

** According to package directions*

SOUPS, BROTHS & CHOWDERS, 8-ounce cup, except as noted

See also Chapter 6

CALORIES

bean, w/smoked ham, canned (Great American) 201
bean, black, canned (Pepperidge Farm) 113
beef, w/barley, mix, prepared* (Wyler's) 72
beef, w/beef chunks and vegetables, canned (Campbell's Chunky) 193
beef, w/noodles, and dumplings, canned (Great American) 109
bouillon, onion, 1 cube, prepared* (Wyler's) 10
broth:
  beef, 1 tsp. prepared* (Maggi Broth & Seasoning) 27
  beef, 1 packet, prepared* (MBT Prime) 8
  chicken, 1 tsp., prepared* (Maggi Broth & Seasoning) 29
  chicken, 1 packet, prepared* (MBT) 10
  clam, 1 tsp., prepared* (Maggi Broth & Seasoning) 30

broth, continued

onion, 1 tsp., prepared* (Maggi Broth & Seasoning) 28
vegetable, 1 tsp., prepared* (Maggi Broth & Seasoning) 27
vegetable, 1 packet, prepared* (MBT) 8

chicken:
w/chicken chunks and vegetables, canned (Campbell's Chunky) 162
cream of, canned (Great American) 108
curry, canned (Pepperidge Farm), ½ can 114
egg drop, frozen, prepared* (Temple) 51
gumbo, creole-style, canned (Great American) 96
w/noodle rings, canned, prepared* (Campbell's Noodle-O's) 70
w/noodle rings, mix, prepared* (Lipton's Ring-O) 58
w/noodles and dumplings, canned (Great American) 89
w/wild rice, canned (Pepperidge Farm), ½ can 58
w/rice and mushrooms, canned (Great American) 96

chili, w/beef, canned (Great American) 179

chowder:
clam, Manhattan, canned (Great American) 111
clam, Manhattan, canned, prepared* (Snow's) 58
clam, New England, canned, prepared* (Campbell's) 155
clam, New England, canned (Pepperidge Farm) 143
sea food, New England, canned, prepared* (Snow's) 147

clam stew, cream of, canned, prepared* (Snow's) 196
consommé, Madrilene, canned (Pepperidge Farm) 66
consommé, w/noodles, mix, prepared* (Knorr Swiss Celestine) 53
hunter's, canned (Pepperidge Farm), ½ can 84
leek, mix, prepared* (Knorr Swiss) 73
lentil, canned, prepared* (Rokeach) 165
lentil, w/ham, canned (Crosse & Blackwell) 258
lobster bisque, w/sherry, canned (Crosse & Blackwell) 117
lobster bisque, w/sherry, canned (Pepperidge Farm), ½ can 151
luk-shen, frozen, prepared* (Temple) 65
minestrone, canned (Crosse & Blackwell) 126
mushroom, cream of, canned (Great American) 131
mushroom, w/white wine, canned (Pepperidge Farm), ½ can 53
noodles, w/chicken flavor, mix, prepared* (Knorr Swiss) 53
onion, mix, prepared* (Knorr Swiss) 40
oxtail, mix, prepared* (Knorr Swiss) 71
oxtail, w/sherry, canned (Crosse & Blackwell) 180
oyster stew, canned (Chicken of the Sea) 163
pea, split, canned, prepared* (Rokeach) 131
pea, split, w/smoked ham, canned (Great American) 186
Petite Marmite, canned (Pepperidge Farm), ½ can 51

tomato:
  canned (Great American) 168
  canned, prepared* (Rokeach) 61
  w/beef and noodles, canned, prepared* (Campbell's Noodle-O's) 120
  w/rice, canned, prepared* (Rokeach) 79
  w/vegetables, canned (Great American) 126
turkey:
  w/turkey chunks and vegetables, canned (Campbell's Chunky) 117
  w/noodles, canned (Great American) 97
  w/rice and mushrooms, canned (Great American) 101
  w/vegetables, canned (Great American) 98
vegetable:
  w/beef broth, canned (Great American) 144
  w/beef stock, canned (Campbell's Chunky) 92
  w/beef, canned (Great American) 126
  w/ground beef, canned (Great American) 139
  w/noodles, canned prepared* (Campbell's Noodle-O's) 74
vegetarian vegetable, canned (Great American) 125
vegetarian vegetable, canned, prepared* (Rokeach) 63
vegetarian vegetable, mix, prepared* (Knorr Swiss) 38
vermicelli, w/meatballs, mix, prepared* (Knorr Swiss) 64
vichyssoise, canned (Crosse & Blackwell) 124
vichyssoise, canned (Pepperidge Farm) 115
won ton, frozen, prepared* (Temple) 78

* *According to package directions*

FANCY VEGETABLES, ½ cup, except as noted

See also Chapter 7

CALORIES

asparagus, in Hollandaise sauce, frozen (Birds Eye), ⅓ pkg. 97
asparagus, cuts and tips, in butter sauce, frozen (Green Giant) 71
beans, baked, w/pork, in molasses sauce, canned (Green Giant) 144
beans, baked, w/pork, in tomato sauce, canned (Green Giant) 135
beans, baked-style, in tomato sauce:
  canned (Stokely-Van Camp) 136
  w/frankfurters, canned (Hormel Mini-Meal), 7½-oz. can 273
  w/frankfurters, canned (Stokely-Van Camp Beanee Weenee) 173
  w/pork, canned (Campbell's Home Style) 149

beans, baked-style, in tomato sauce, continued

w/pork, canned (Stokely-Van Camp) 138
beans, green, French-style, in butter sauce, frozen (Green Giant) 95
beans, green, French-style, in mushroom sauce, frozen (Green Giant) 67
beans, lima, baby, in butter sauce, frozen (Green Giant) 135
beets, Harvard, canned (Stokely-Van Camp) 55
beets, pickled, canned (Stokely-Van Camp) 77
beets, sliced, in orange flavor glaze, frozen (Birds Eye) 53
broccoli spears, in butter sauce, frozen (Green Giant) 59
broccoli spears, in Hollandaise sauce, frozen (Birds Eye) 100
broccoli cuts, in cheese sauce, frozen (Green Giant) 67
Brussels sprouts, in butter sauce, frozen (Green Giant) 69
carrot nuggets, in butter sauce, frozen (Green Giant) 54
cauliflower au gratin, frozen (Stouffer's), 10-oz. pkg. 318
cauliflower, in butter sauce, frozen (Green Giant) 45
cauliflower, in cheese sauce, frozen (Green Giant) 83
corn, in butter sauce, frozen (Green Giant) 97
corn, white, in butter sauce, frozen (Green Giant) 106
corn, w/peppers, in butter sauce, frozen (Green Giant) 107
corn fritters, fried, frozen (Mrs. Paul's), 12-oz. pkg. 846
corn soufflé, frozen (Stouffer's), 12-oz. pkg. 492
eggplant Parmesan, frozen (Mrs. Paul's), 11-oz. pkg. 632
eggplant sticks, breaded, fried, frozen (Mrs. Paul's), 7-oz. pkg. 516
mushrooms, whole, in butter sauce, frozen (Green Giant) 65
onions, in cream sauce, frozen (Green Giant) 54
onions, French-fried rings, frozen (Ore-Ida), 4 average 123
peas, early, in butter sauce, frozen (Green Giant Le Sueur) 87
peas, sweet, in butter sauce, frozen (Green Giant) 91
peas, w/onions, in butter sauce, frozen (Green Giant) 97
potato pancakes, mix, prepared** (French's), 3 small 90
potatoes:

au gratin, frozen (Stouffer's), 11½-oz. pkg. 301
au gratin, mix, prepared** (Betty Crocker) 160
au gratin, mix, prepared** (French's) 112
boiled, buttered, w/parsley, frozen (Seabrook Farms) 104
baked, stuffed, w/cheese topping, frozen
(Holloway House), 12-oz. pkg. 502
baked, stuffed, w/sour cream, frozen
(Holloway House), 12-oz. pkg. 511
French-fried, frozen (Birds Eye Fanci-Fries), ¼ pkg. 173
French-fried, frozen (Ore-Ida Cottage Fries), 17 pieces 141
French-fried, frozen (Ore-Ida Golden Crinkles), 17 pieces 102

French-fried, frozen (Ore-Ida Golden Fries), 17 pieces 97
French-fried, frozen (Ore-ida Shoestring), 25 pieces 70
French-fried, bites, frozen (Ore-Ida Tater Tots), 10 pieces 168
mashed, mix, prepared** (Betty Crocker Potato Buds) 134
mashed, mix, prepared** (Ore-Ida Potato Flakes) 132
mashed, mix, prepared** (Pillsbury) 137
scalloped, frozen (Stouffer's), 12-oz. pkg. 389
scalloped, mix, prepared** (Betty Crocker) 150
scalloped, mix, prepared** (French's) 109
scalloped, w/ham, canned (Hormel Mini-Meal), 7½-oz. can 241
and peas, creamed, frozen (Stouffer's), 10-oz. pkg. 325
potatoes, sweet, in syrup, canned (Green Giant) 99
potatoes, sweet, w/brown sugar pineapple glaze, frozen* (Birds Eye) ... 145
sauerkraut, w/caraway, canned (Stokely-Van Camp Bavarian Style) 24
spinach, leaf, in butter sauce, frozen (Green Giant) 137
spinach, creamed, frozen* (Birds Eye), ⅓ pkg. 62
spinach soufflé, frozen (Stouffer's), 12-oz. pkg. 484
spinach soufflé, frozen (Swanson), 7½-oz. pkg. 260
succotash, cream-style, canned (Stokely-Van Camp) 87
tomato aspic, canned (Stokely-Van Camp) 20
vegetables, mixed, frozen:
in butter sauce (Green Giant) 67
in cream sauce* (Birds Eye Vegetable Jubilee) 138
Bavarian style, in sauce (Birds Eye International), ⅓ pkg. 138
Danish style, in sauce (Birds Eye International), ⅓ pkg. 90
Hawaiian style, in sauce (Birds Eye International), ⅓ pkg. 99
Japanese style, in sauce (Birds Eye International), ⅓ pkg. 100
Mexican style, in sauce (Birds Eye International), ⅓ pkg. 203
Parisian style, in sauce (Birds Eye International), ⅓ pkg. 75
Spanish style, in sauce (Birds Eye International), ⅓ pkg. 83
zucchini, breaded, fried, frozen (Mrs. Paul's), 9-oz. pkg. 566
zucchini Parmesan, frozen (Mrs. Paul's), 12-oz. pkg. 259

* *Without butter added*
** *According to package directions*

FROZEN DINNERS, 1 complete dinner*

See also Chapter 9 and "Frozen Entrees"

	CALORIES
beans and franks (Swanson "TV"), 11½ oz.	610
beef (Morton—3-course), 17 oz.	520
beef (Swanson "TV"), 11 oz.	414
beef (Swanson "TV"—3-course), 16 oz.	592
beef, chopped (Swanson "TV"), 10 oz.	447
chicken, fried (Morton—3-course), 17 oz.	723
chicken, fried (Swanson "TV"), 11½ oz.	575
chicken, fried (Swanson "TV"—3-course), 16 oz.	652
chicken and dumplings (Morton—3-course), 16½ oz.	820
Chinese (Swanson "TV" International), 11 oz.	356
Chinese (Temple), 12 oz.	340
chop suey, beef (Banquet), 11 oz.	287
chow mein:	
beef (Chun King), 11 oz.	389
chicken (Banquet), 11 oz.	291
chicken (Chun King), 11 oz.	352
shrimp (Chun King), 11 oz.	378
egg foo young (Chun King), 11 oz.	403
enchilada, beef (Patio), 12 oz.	757
enchilada, cheese (Patio), 12 oz.	591
fish, ocean, filet of (Swanson "TV"), 12¼ oz.	397
fish, perch, ocean (Banquet), 8.8 oz.	472
fish, and French fries (Swanson "TV"), 9¾ oz.	429
German (Swanson "TV" International), 11 oz.	405
ham (Swanson "TV"), 10¼ oz.	366
Italian (Swanson "TV" International), 13½ oz.	428
loin of pork (Swanson "TV"), 10 oz.	460
macaroni and beef (Swanson "TV"), 11¼ oz.	302
macaroni and cheese (Swanson "TV"), 12¾ oz.	367
meat loaf (Morton—3-course), 17 oz.	573
meat loaf (Swanson "TV"), 10¾ oz.	450
meat loaf (Swanson "TV"—3-course), 16½ oz.	510
Mexican (Patio), 15 oz.	722
Mexican (Swanson "TV" International), 16 oz.	647
Mexican Combination (Patio), 12 oz.	683
noodles and chicken (Swanson "TV"), 11 oz.	378

Salisbury steak (Morton—3-course), 17 oz.	573
Salisbury steak (Swanson "TV"—3-course), 17 oz.	520
shrimp, fried (Swanson "TV"), 8 oz.	381
spaghetti and meatballs (Swanson "TV"), 12 oz.	357
Swiss steak (Swanson "TV"), 10 oz.	361
turkey (Morton—3-course), 17 oz.	615
turkey (Swanson "TV"), 11½ oz.	377
turkey (Swanson "TV"—3-course), 17½ oz.	557

* *Note variations in size*

PACKAGED DINNER MIXES, 1 cup, prepared*

See also Chapter 10 and "Frozen Entrees"

	CALORIES
macaroni:	
and cheese (Kraft Dinner)	350
and cheese (Kraft Deluxe Dinner)	324
w/chili flavor sauce (Kraft Mexican Style Dinner)	302
w/Italian style sauce (Kraft Italian Style Dinner)	266
w/tomato chili sauce (Betty Crocker Macaroni Monte Bello)	350
noodles:	
and cheese (Kraft Dinner)	464
w/cheese sauce and ham (Lipton Ham Cheddarton)	264
w/chicken and sauce (Kraft Noodles with Chicken Dinner)	298
w/chicken sauce and almonds (Betty Crocker Noodles Almondine)	426
w/Italian style sauce (Betty Crocker Noodles Italiano)	414
w/sour cream and cheese sauce (Betty Crocker Noodles Romanoff)	482
w/sour cream and cheese sauce (Kraft Noodles Romanoff)	478
w/soy-celery sauce and almonds (Betty Crocker Noodles Cantong)	403
w/Stroganoff sauce (Betty Crocker Noodles Stroganoff)	500
w/Stroganoff sauce and chicken (Lipton Chicken Stroganoff)	310
rice, w/chicken and sauce (Lipton Chicken Supreme)	271
spaghetti (Kraft Mild American Style Dinner)	292
spaghetti (Kraft Tangy Italian Style Dinner)	276
spaghetti, w/meat sauce (Kraft Deluxe Spaghetti Dinner)	360
taco casserole (McCormick Dinner Mexicana)	400
tamale pie (McCormick Dinner Mexicana)	470

* *According to package directions*

FROZEN ENTREES, 1 whole package*

See also Chapters 8, 9 and 10

	CALORIES
beef and noodles (Morton Casserole), 9 oz.	336
beef, chipped, creamed (Banquet Cookin' Bag), 5 oz.	127
beef, chipped, creamed (Stouffer's), 5¾ oz.	287
beef, chipped, creamed (Swanson Pouch), 5¾ oz.	311
beef pot pie:	
(Banquet—family size), 36 oz.	1311
(Morton), 8 oz.	372
(Stouffer's), 10 oz.	554
(Swanson Deep Dish), 16 oz.	631
beef ragout (Swanson Pouch), 8½ oz.	177
beef stew (Banquet Buffet Supper), 32 oz.	720
beef Stroganoff (Swanson Pouch), 6½ oz.	213
cabbage, beef-stuffed (Holloway House), 14 oz.	368
cheese soufflé (Stouffer's), 12 oz.	730
chicken and dumplings (Banquet Buffet Supper), 32 oz.	1306
chicken and noodles (Banquet Buffet Supper), 32 oz.	736
chicken and noodles (Swanson Tray), 8 oz.	285
chicken, breast of, in gravy (Stouffer's), 12 oz.	667
chicken, in cream sauce (Swanson Pouch), 6 oz.	243
chicken, creamed (Stouffer's), 6½ oz.	344
chicken, fried:	
(Banquet Entree), 14 oz.	960
(Banquet Entree), 32 oz.	2195
(Morton Chicken in a Basket), 32 oz.	1984
and whipped potatoes (Swanson "TV" Entree), 7 oz.	412
chicken, escalloped, and noodles (Morton Casserole), 9 oz.	517
chicken, escalloped, and noodles (Stouffer's), 11½ oz.	587
chicken pot pie (Stouffer's), 10 oz.	561
chicken pot pie (Swanson Deep Dish), 16 oz.	731
chili con carne, w/beans (Banquet Cookin' Bag), 8 oz.	310
chop suey, beef (Banquet Cookin' Bag), 7 oz.	121
chop suey, beef (Banquet Buffet Supper), 32 oz.	554
chow mein:	
beef (Chun King), 15 oz.	268
chicken (Banquet Cookin' Bag), 7 oz.	123
chicken (Banquet Buffet Supper), 32 oz.	563

chicken (Chun King), 15 oz. 326
chicken (Stouffer's), 28 oz. 528
chicken (Temple), 12 oz. 194
chicken (Temple), 32 oz. 518
shrimp (Chun King), 15 oz. 190
shrimp (Temple), 12 oz. 199
shrimp (Temple), 32 oz. 531
vegetables (Temple), 12 oz. 102
vegetable (Temple), 32 oz. 272
clams, breaded, fried (Mrs. Paul's), 5 oz. 505
crab, deviled, precooked (Mrs. Paul's Miniatures), 7 oz. 422
crab, King Alaska, Newburg (Stouffer's), 6½ oz. 312
enchiladas, beef, w/sauce (Banquet Cookin' Bag), 6 oz. 259
enchiladas, beef, w/gravy (Patio), 22 oz. 1480
enchiladas, cheese (Patio), 8 oz. 259
fish and chips (Gorton's English-Style), 16 oz. 785
fish and chips (Mrs. Paul's American-Style), 14 oz. 708
fish cakes, breaded, precooked (Mrs. Paul's Sandwich Thins), 10 oz. 552
fish fillets, buttered, precooked (Mrs. Paul's), 10 oz. 376
fish fillets, breaded, fried (Mrs. Paul's), 8 oz. 415
fish fillets, breaded, French-fried (Gorton's Fish Crisps), 8 oz. 500
fish puffs, in English batter, precooked (Gorton's), 8 oz. 465
fish sticks, breaded, precooked (Gorton's), 8 oz. 400
flounder, almondine, precooked (Gorton's), 8 oz. 470
hash, roast beef (Stouffer's), 11½ oz. 471
lasagne, w/meat sauce (Stouffer's), 30 oz. 1316
lobster, Newburg (Stouffer's), 6½ oz. 377
macaroni and beef (Morton Casserole), 9 oz. 290
macaroni and beef w/tomatoes (Stouffer's), 11½ oz. 413
macaroni and beef w/tomato sauce (Kraft), 11½ oz. 449
macaroni and cheese:
(Howard Johnson—family size), 20 oz. 1100
(Kraft), 12½ oz. 613
(Morton—family size), 20 oz. 733
(Stouffer's), 12 oz. 480
(Stouffer's—family size), 26 oz. 1040
(Swanson), 8 oz. 328
meat loaf (Banquet Cookin' Bag), 5 oz. 281
meat loaf (Kraft), 24 oz. 1584
meat loaf and whipped potatoes (Swanson "TV" Entree), 9¼ oz. 329
noodles Romanoff (Stouffer's), 12 oz. 549
peppers, beef-stuffed (Holloway House), 14 oz. 355

frozen entrees, continued

pork, sweet and sour, w/vegetables and sauce (Chun King), 14 oz. 676
Salisbury steak, with gravy:
(Banquet Cookin' Bag), 5 oz. 239
(Banquet Buffet Supper), 32 oz. 1524
(Holloway House), 14 oz. 640
and crinkle cut potatoes (Swanson "TV" Entree), 6 oz. 360
scallops, in lemon butter (Gorton's), 9 oz. 520
shrimp cakes, breaded, precooked (Mrs. Paul's), 6 oz. 315
shrimp scampi (Gorton's), 7½ oz. 640
shrimp, w/lobster sauce and rice (Temple), 12 oz. 222
Sloppy Joe (Stouffer's), 26 oz. 1020
sole fillets, in lemon butter, precooked (Gorton's), 9 oz. 470
spaghetti and meat (Morton Casserole), 8 oz. 232
spaghetti, with meat sauce:
(Banquet Cookin' Bag), 8 oz. 323
(Banquet Entree), 8 oz. 310
(Kraft), 12½ oz. 338
(Swanson Pouch), 8 oz. 233
Swiss steak, w/gravy (Stouffer's), 10 oz. 583
Swiss steak, w/gravy (Holloway House), 14 oz. 471
swordfish, in lemon butter, precooked (Gorton's), 9 oz. 430
tacos, beef (Patio), 13½ oz. 1074
tamales, w/sauce (Banquet Cookin' Bag), 6 oz. 219
tamales, w/gravy (Patio), 20 oz. 1400
tuna noodle casserole (Stouffer's), 11½ oz. 448
turkey, w/gravy and whipped potatoes (Swanson "TV" Entree), 8¾ oz. ..292
turkey pot pie (Banquet—family size), 36 oz. 1529
turkey tetrazzini (Stouffer's), 12 oz. 713
veal Parmigiana (Kraft), 13 oz. 559
veal, breaded, w/spaghetti (Swanson "TV" Entree), 8¼ oz. 272
Welsh rarebit (Stouffer's), 10 oz. 737

* *Note variations in size*

CANNED ENTREES

See also Chapters 8, 9 and 10

CALORIES
beef brisket, corned, cooked (Festival Main Meal Meat), 8 oz. 361
beef brisket, corned, cooked (Wilson's Certified Tender Made), 8 oz. 361

beef goulash (Hormel Mini-Meal), 7½-oz. can 224
beef roast, cooked (Festival Main Meal Meat), 8 oz. 267
beef roast, cooked (Wilson's Certified Tender Made), 8 oz. 267
beef roast, w/gravy (Armour Star), 8 oz. 290
beef stew (Austex), 1 cup 226
beef stew (Broadcast), 1 cup 246
beef stew (Libby's), 1 cup 217
chili con carne, see Mexican Foods, pages 53-54
chow mein, see Chinese Foods, pages 52-53
clams, creamed, w/mushrooms (Snow's), 1 cup 254
corned beef hash (Austex), 1 cup 446
corned beef hash (Libby's), 1 cup 444
corned beef hash (Libby's Home Style), 1 cup 510
ham, cooked, 8 oz.:
  (Armour Star) 416
  (Armour Star Golden Star) 304
  (Armour Star Parti Style) 336
  (Festival) 386
  (Festival Main Meal Meat) 344
  (Wilson's Certified) 386
  (Wilson's Certified Tender Made) 344
ham, smoked, see "Frankfurters, Sausage & Smoked Meats," page 142
ham and lima beans (Austex), 1 cup 232
noodles w/sour cream and beef (Hormel Mini-Meal), 7½-oz. can 237
pork roast, cooked (Festival Main Meal Meat), 8 oz. 354
pork roast, cooked (Wilson's Certified Tender Made), 8 oz. 354
Sloppy Joe, w/barbecue sauce (Libby's), 1 cup 352
Sloppy Joe, w/pizza sauce, pepperoni and cheese (Libby's), 1 cup 384
spaghetti, 1 cup:
  w/ground beef and tomato sauce (Chef Boy-Ar-Dee Pizzaghetti) 188
  w/meat balls and tomato sauce (Austex) 298
  w/meat balls and tomato sauce (Chef Boy-Ar-Dee Beefoghetti) 221
  w/tomato sauce (Stokely-Van Camp) 210
turkey roast, cooked (Festival Main Meal Meat), 8 oz. 234
turkey roast, cooked (Wilson's Certified Tender Made), 8 oz. 234
turkey roast, cooked, w/dressing (Festival Main Meal Meat), 8 oz. 424
Welsh rarebit (Snow's), 1 cup 384
Welsh rarebit, w/sherry (Snow's), 1 cup 324

FRANKFURTERS, SAUSAGES & SMOKED MEATS*

See also Chapter 8

	CALORIES
frankfurters:	
pure beef (Vienna Beefsteak Wieners), 1-lb. pkg.	1126
all beef (Festival), 1-lb. pkg.	1358
all beef (Wilson's Certified), 1-lb. pkg.	1358
all meat (Armour Star Hot Dogs), 1-lb. pkg.	1420
all meat (Festival Skinless), 1-lb. pkg.	1398
all meat (Morrell Pride), 1-lb. pkg.	1462
all meat (Oscar Mayer Imperial Size), 1-lb. pkg.	1400
all meat (Oscar Mayer Little Wieners), 5½-oz. pkg.	480
all meat (Wilson's Certified Skinless), 1-lb. pkg.	1398
all meat (Yorkshire), 1-lb. pkg.	1466
ham, cured, smoked, cooked, 8-oz. serving:	
(Oscar Mayer Jubilee, Bone-in)	632
(Festival, Boneless)	382
(Morrell's Chef Brand, Boneless)	426
(Oscar Mayer Jubilee Slice, Boneless)	344
(Wilson's Certified Boneless)	382
knockwurst, pure beef (Vienna), 12-oz. pkg.	989
knockwurst, all meat (Oscar Mayer Chubbies), 12-oz. pkg.	1050
pork loin, smoked, canned (Festival Main Meal Meat), 8 oz.	304
pork shoulder, smoked (Wilson's Certified Smoked Picnic), 8 oz.	558
pork shoulder butt, smoked (Oscar Mayer Sweet Morsel), 8 oz.	712
sausage, breakfast, pure beef (Vienna), 8-oz. pkg., cooked	328
sausage, Polish, pure beef (Vienna), 12-oz. pkg.	1129
sausage, Polish, all meat (Oscar Mayer), 12-oz. pkg.	960
sausage, pork, fresh (raw when purchased):	
links (Morrell Pride Tasty Skinless), 12-oz. pkg., cooked	720
patties (Oscar Mayer), 12-oz. box, cooked	600
roll (Morrell Pride), 1-lb. pkg., cooked	965
roll (Oscar Mayer—regular or hot), 1-lb. pkg., cooked	608
sausage, smokie link:	
(Eckrich Smokies), 12-oz. pkg.	1150
(Eckrich Smokettes), 10-oz. pkg.	900
(Eckrich Smok-Y-Links), 10-oz. pkg.	900
(Festival Smokies), 12-oz. pkg.	1005
(Oscar Mayer Little Smokies), 5-oz. pkg.	464

(Oscar Mayer Smoked Breakfast Sausage), 5-oz. pkg. 462

* *Note variations in package sizes—and bear in mind that when sausages are packaged in uniform size links, you can calculate the calories in a single link simply by dividing the caloric content of the whole package by the number of links it contains.*

LUNCHEON MEATS & SPREADS*

See also Chapter 8

CALORIES

beef, corned (Leo's), 3½-oz. pkg. 116
beef, corned, spread (Underwood), 1 tbsp. 27
beef, pepper (Vienna), 4-oz. pkg. 176
beef, roasted (Leo's Roast Beef), 3½-oz. pkg. 75
beef, chopped, pressed:
(Danola Sandwich Beef), 4-oz. pkg. 122
(Eckrich Slender Sliced), 3-oz. pkg. 114
corned (Eckrich Slender Sliced), 3-oz. pkg. 120
corned (Leo's), 3-oz. pkg. 109
corned (Oscar Mayer Thin-Sliced), 4-oz. pkg. 156
smoked (Carl Buddig) 3-oz. pkg. 103
smoked (Leo's), 3-oz. pkg. 109
smoked (Leo's Ripple Pack), 5-oz. pkg. 181
smoked (Oscar Mayer Thin-Sliced), 4-oz. pkg. 156
smoked, spicy (Leo's), 3-oz. pkg. 109
bologna:
pure beef (Eckrich), 6-oz. pkg. 510
all meat (Eckrich), 8-oz. pkg. 739
all meat (Eckrich Sandwich), 8-oz. pkg. 674
all meat (Eckrich German), 8-oz. pkg. 630
all meat (Festival), 8-oz. pkg. 699
all meat (Morrell Pride), 6-oz. pkg. 532
all meat (Wilson's Certified), 8-oz. pkg. 699
all meat, ring style (Oscar Mayer), 1-lb. ring 1459
all meat, ring style (Oscar Mayer Wisconsin), 1-lb. ring 1232
braunschweiger:
(Eckrich), 8-oz. pkg. 568
(Festival), 8-oz. pkg. 716
(Morrell Pride), 8-oz. pkg. 655
(Wilson's Certified), 8-oz. pkg. 716
chicken, breast of, loaf (Eckrich), 6-oz. pkg. 193
chicken, chopped, pressed (Eckrich Slender Sliced), 3-oz. pkg. 131

chicken, smoked, chopped, pressed (Leo's), 3-oz. pkg. 144
chili con carne spread, w/o beans (Oscar Mayer), 1 tbsp. 26
chili con carne spread, w/beans (Oscar Mayer), 1 tbsp. 31
gourmet loaf (Eckrich), 8-oz. pkg. 227
ham, boiled or cooked:
(Leo's—imported), 4-oz. rectangular pkg. 98
(Leo's—imported), 4-oz. square pkg. 144
(Leo's), 4-oz. pkg. 213
(Plumrose), 4-oz. pkg. 114
smoked (Oscar Mayer), 5-oz. pkg. 215
ham, minced (Oscar Mayer), 8-oz. pkg. 544
ham, smoked, chopped, pressed (Eckrich Slender Sliced), 3-oz. pkg. . . . 140
ham, smoked, chopped, pressed (Leo's), 3-oz. pkg. 144
ham, smoked, chopped, pressed (Oscar Mayer Thin-Sliced), 4-oz. pkg. . . 156
ham spread, deviled (Hormel), 1 tbsp. 38
ham spread, deviled (Plumrose), 1 tbsp. 43
ham and cheese spread (Oscar Mayer Roll), 1 tbsp. 33
ham salad spread (Oscar Mayer), 1 tbsp. 24
honey seasoned loaf (Eckrich), 8-oz. pkg. 335
liver sausage, ring style (Oscar Mayer), 12-oz. ring 1052
luncheon meat loaf, pure beef (Oscar Mayer), 8-oz. pkg. 568
luncheon meat loaf, all meat (Eckrich), 8-oz. pkg. 320
luncheon meat spread, deviled (Deviled Treet), 1 tbsp. 44
luncheon roll sausage (Oscar Mayer), 8-oz. pkg. 264
pastrami, all beef (Leo's), 3½-oz. pkg. 139
pastrami, smoked, chopped, pressed (Leo's), 3-oz. pkg. 109
peppered loaf (Eckrich), 8-oz. pkg. 301
pickle and pimiento loaf (Morrell Pride), 6-oz. pkg. 396
potted meat spread (Libby's), 1 tbsp. 35
salami, all meat, cooked (Eckrich), 8-oz. pkg. 465
salami, all meat, cooked (Morrell Pride), 6-oz. pkg. 396
sandwich spread (Oscar Mayer), 1 tbsp. 21
thuringer spread, smoked (Oscar Mayer Smoky Snax), 1 tbsp. 51
tongue, pure beef (Vienna), 4-oz. pkg. 284
turkey, breast of (Leo's), 3½-oz. pkg. 98
turkey, smoked, chopped, pressed:
(Eckrich Slender Sliced), 3-oz. pkg. 114
(Leo's Breast of Turkey), 3-oz. pkg. 118
(Leo's Dark Turkey), 3-oz. pkg. 135
(Oscar Mayer Thin-Sliced Turkey Breast), 4-oz. pkg. 120

** Note variations in package sizes—and bear in mind that if luncheon meat is packaged in uniform-size slices, you can calculate the calories in a single slice by following this easy formula: just divide the caloric content of the whole package by the number of slices it contains.*

FROZEN PIZZA, 1 whole pie*

See also Chapter 9

	CALORIES
cheese:	
(Jeno's), 12½ oz.	808
(Jeno's Jr's), 2½ oz.	164
(Kraft), 14 oz.	826
(Kraft Pee Wee), 2½ oz.	169
(Roman), 15 oz.	891
hamburger (Jeno's), 13¼ oz.	850
pepperoni (Chef Boy-Ar-Dee Little), 2¾ oz.	176
pepperoni (Jeno's), 13¼ oz.	1008
pepperoni (Roman), 15 oz.	1084
sausage:	
(Jeno's), 13¼ oz.	910
(Jeno's Jr's), 2½ oz.	173
(Kraft), 14½ oz.	999
(Kraft Pee Wee), 2½ oz.	191

** Note variations in size*

FROZEN SNACKS & HORS D'OEUVRES, 1 piece*

See also Chapter 18

	CALORIES
burrito rolls, bean and bacon (Patio)	47
burrito rolls, beef (Patio)	48
burrito rolls, chicken (Patio)	50
egg rolls:	
chicken, cocktail size (Chun King)	28
lobster and meat, cocktail size (Chun King)	26
meat and shrimp, cocktail size (Chun King)	29
meat and shrimp, medium size (Chun King), 1-oz. piece	46
shrimp, cocktail size (Chun King)	24
shrimp, large size (Chun King), 2½-oz. piece	145
shrimp, large size (Temple), 2½-oz. piece	118
pizza rolls:	
cheeseburger (Jeno's)	41

pizza rolls, continued

pepperoni (Jenó's) 40
sausage (Jeno's) 40
shrimp (Jeno's) 34
Sloppy Joe (Jeno's) 35

logs, fish and chip (Jeno's Snack Logs), 2-oz. piece 157
logs, Reuben (Jeno's Snack Logs), 2-oz. piece 136
logs, sausage pizza (Jeno's Snack Logs), 2-oz. piece 153
puffs, chicken (Durkee) 50
puffs, chicken liver (Durkee) 48
puffs, shrimp (Durkee) 44
tacos, beef, cocktail size (Patio) 39

** ½ ounce each, except as noted*

APPETIZERS & HORS D'OEUVRES, CANNED OR IN JARS

See also Chapters 8 and 18

CALORIES

anchovies, flat (Reese), 2-oz. can 100
caviar:

black, sturgeon (Northland Queen), 1 oz. 74
black, sturgeon (Romanoff Iranian), 1 oz. 74
red, salmon (Cascade Brand), 1 oz. 68
red, salmon (Romanoff), 1 oz. 68
red, salmon (Romar Brand), 1 oz. 68

chicken livers, chopped (Reese), 1 oz. 47
fish balls (King Oscar), 14-oz. can 137
frankfurters, cocktail (Vienna), 1 oz. 88
gefilte fish, cocktail (Manischewitz Fishlets), 1 piece 7
gefilte fish, cocktail (Manischewitz Deluxe Fishlets), 1 piece 6
herring:

kippered (King Oscar), 8-oz. can 480
kippered (King Oscar Kipper Snacks), 3¾-oz. can 205
pickled (Vita Cocktail), 8-oz. jar 344
pickled (Vita Lunch), 8-oz. jar 480
pickled (Vita Matjes), 8-oz. jar 304
pickled, in wine sauce (Vita Party Snacks), 8-oz. jar 400
pickled, in wine sauce (Vita Tastee Bits), 8-oz. jar 360

mushrooms, cocktail (Cresca), 3-oz. jar 16
mushrooms, cocktail (Reese Buttons), 4-oz. jar, drained 25

mussels, in natural juice (Cresca), 1 cup 160
oysters, smoked (Reese), 3¾-oz. can 259
pâté (Cresca Pâté Au Foie), 1 oz. 103
pâté (Cresca Pâté Maison), 1 oz. 110
pâté (Cresca Smoked Goose Pâté), 1 oz. 123
salami, Danish (Cresca), 1 oz. 130
salami, Danish (Reese Sticks), 1 oz. 128
salmon, smoked, lox (Vita), 4-oz. tin 136
salmon, smoked, Nova Scotia (Vita), 4-oz. tin 220
sardines, Norwegian Brislings (Reese), 3¾-oz. can 330
sardines, Portuguese (Reese), 3¾-oz. can 330
sausage, Vienna (Armour Star), 1 sausage 45
sausage, Vienna (Libby's Home-Style), 1 sausage 50
sausage, Vienna (Wilson's Certified), 1 sausage 48
shrimp (Cresca Tiny), 1 oz. 30
shrimp (Pacific Pearl Tiny), 1 oz. 25

DIPS, READY-TO-EAT, 8-ounce foil tin, except as noted

See also Chapter 18

CALORIES

bacon and horseradish (Borden's), 4-oz. tin 316
bacon and horseradish (Kraft Teez) 456
bacon and smoke flavor (Sealtest Dip 'n Dressing) 379
blue cheese (Kraft Teez) 408
clam (Kraft Teez) 360
clam and lobster (Borden's), 4-oz. tin 240
garden spice (Borden's), 4-oz. tin 264
garlic (Kraft Teez) 376
green chili (Borden's) 442
green goddess (Kraft Teez) 368
jalapeno bean (Old El Paso), 7½-oz. can 263
onion:
  French (Borden's), 4-oz. tin 284
  French (Borden's—sour cream base) 472
  French (Kraft Teez) 344
  French (Sealtest Dip 'n Dressing) 378
onion and garlic (Sealtest Dip 'n Dressing) 367

CHIPS, CRISPS & RELATED SNACKS, 1 ounce

See also Chapter 17

	CALORIES
chips:	
bacon flavored (Parker)	149
corn (Frito-Lay Fandangos)	164
corn, popped (Frito-Lay Intermission)	153
potato (Nabisco Chipsters)	136
potato (Wonder)	158
potato, barbecue flavored (Wonder)	154
taco-tortilla (Wonder)	148
tortilla (Wonder)	144
crisps:	
barbecue flavored (General Mills Barbecue Vittles)	134
corn (Wonder Corn Capers)	158
(Nabisco Doo Dads)	143
martini (Parker)	161
pizza (General Mills Pizza Spins)	144
pizza (Wise Pizza Wheels)	140
potato (Frito-Lay Munchos)	152
potato, French fried (General Mills)	156
rings, onion flavored (Frito-Lay Funyuns)	145
rings, onion flavored (Wise)	133
rings, onion flavored (Wonder)	133

SALAD DRESSINGS, 1 tablespoon

See also Chapter 11

	CALORIES
blue cheese:	
bottled (Bernstein's of Long Beach)	57
bottled (Kraft Imperial)	60
bottled (Kraft Refrigerated)	75
bottled (Wishbone French-style)	63
mix, prepared* (Good Seasons Thick 'n Creamy)	89
Caesar, bottled (Kraft Golden)	60
Caesar, bottled (Kraft Imperial)	76
Caesar, w/garlic-cheese, mix, prepared* (Lawry's)	83

Cheddar-wine, bottled (Seven Seas) 63
cole slaw, mix, prepared* (Good Seasons Thick 'n Creamy) 91
French:
  bottled (Bernstein's of Long Beach) 62
  bottled (Lawry's) 60
  bottled (Lawry's San Francisco) 53
  bottled (Seven Seas Creole) 58
  bottled (Wishbone Classic French) 63
  mix, prepared* (Good Seasons Riviera) 94
fruit, bottled (Kraft) 59
green goddess:
  bottled (Bernstein's of Long Beach) 59
  bottled (Kraft) 74
  bottled (Kraft Imperial) 80
  mix, prepared* (Good Seasons Thick 'n Creamy) 87
  mix, prepared* (Lawry's) 93
hickory flavor, bottled (Wishbone Hickory Bits) 84
Italian:
  bottled (Bernstein's of Long Beach) 70
  bottled (Lawry's) 79
  bottled (Wishbone Italian Rosé) 63
  mix, prepared* (Good Seasons Mild) 89
  w/cheese, mix, prepared* (Good Seasons Cheese Italian) 89
  w/cheese, mix, prepared* (Lawry's) 83
mayonnaise, bottled (Bama) 95
mayonnaise, bottled (Saffola) 100
mayonnaise-type, bottled (Bama) 59
mayonnaise-type, bottled (Saffola) 52
mayonnaise-type, w/relish, bottled (Kraft Salad and Sandwich) 56
oil and vinegar, bottled (Lawry's Red Wine Vinegar and Oil) 55
onion, bottled, (Wishbone California) 78
onion, bottled (Kraft Green Onion) 71
Parmesan, bottled (Wishbone Parmesano) 66
Roquefort:
  bottled (Bernstein's of Long Beach) 64
  bottled (Kraft Refrigerated) 52
  bottled (Kraft Refrigerated Imperial) 71
  bottled (Reese) 27
Russian, bottled (Kraft Creamy) 70
sweet and sour, bottled (Kraft) 32
Thousand Island:
  bottled (Bernstein's of Long Beach) 59

Thousand Island salad dressing, continued

bottled (Kraft Imperial or Refrigerated)	78
bottled (Kraft Pourable)	57
bottled (Lawry's)	69
mix, prepared* (Good Seasons Thick 'n Creamy)	85
vinegarette, bottled (Bernstein's of Long Beach)	61

** According to package directions*

SAUCES & GRAVIES, ½ cup

See also Chapter 12

	CALORIES
au jus gravy, mix, prepared* (French's)	10
au jus gravy, mix, prepared* (McCormick)	15
barbecue sauce:	
bottled (Cattlemen's Regular)	73
bottled (Cattlemen's Mild)	135
bottled (Kraft)	145
mix, prepared* (Kraft)	147
for chicken, bottled (Compliment)	122
garlic or hickory smoke flavored, bottled (Kraft)	145
Hawaiian, bottled (Chun King)	128
hickory smoke flavored, bottled (Cattlemen's)	153
hot, bottled (Kraft)	144
w/mushroom bits, bottled (Open Pit)	216
w/onion bits, bottled (Kraft)	200
w/onion bits, bottled (Open Pit)	216
for pork, bottled (Compliment)	104
barbecue glaze, bottled (Bernstein's of Long Beach)	380
Bordelaise sauce, canned (Betty Crocker)	66
brown gravy, mix, prepared* (Kraft)	45
brown gravy, mix, prepared* (Pillsbury)	31
brown gravy, herb flavored, mix, prepared* (McCormick)	41
brown gravy, w/onion, canned (Franco-American)	49
cheese sauce, canned (Betty Crocker)	154
cheese sauce, cheddar, mix, prepared* (Kraft)	212
chicken gravy, mix, prepared* (Kraft)	60
chicken gravy, mix, prepared* (Pillsbury)	53
chicken Supreme sauce, canned (Compliment)	118
chop suey sauce, mix, prepared* (Durkee)	51

enchilada sauce, mild or hot, canned (Old El Paso) 49
gravy, canned (Pillsbury Home Style) 29
Hollandaise sauce, canned (Betty Crocker) 168
Hollandaise sauce, mix, prepared* (Kraft) 217
Hollandaise sauce, mix, prepared* (McCormick) 170
Italian sauce, canned (Contadina) 72
meat loaf sauce, canned (Compliment) 109
meat loaf sauce, canned (Contadina) 64
mushroom sauce, canned (Betty Crocker) 72
mushroom sauce, canned (Contadina) 88
Newburg sauce, canned (Betty Crocker) 136
Newburg sauce, w/sherry, canned (Snow's) 129
onion gravy, mix, prepared* (Kraft) 46
pizza sauce, canned (Chef Boy-Ar-Dee) 100
pork gravy, mix, prepared* (French's) 40
pork chop sauce, canned (Compliment) 120
sandwich sauce, wo/meat, canned (Hunt's Manwich) 69
sour cream sauce, mix, prepared* (Kraft) 242
spaghetti sauce:
  meatless, canned (Chef Boy-Ar-Dee) 67
  meatless, in jars (Chef Boy-Ar-Dee Homestyle) 80
  meatless, in jars (Heinz) 98
  meatless, mix, prepared* (Kraft) 66
  w/ground beef, in jars (Chef Boy-Ar-Dee) 151
  w/meat, canned or in jars (Chef Boy-Ar-Dee) 113
  w/meat, in jars (Heinz) 110
  w/meat and mushrooms, in jars (Heinz) 107
  w/meatballs, canned or in jars (Chef Boy-Ar-Dee) 117
  w/mushrooms, canned (Chef Boy-Ar-Dee) 77
  w/mushrooms, in jars (Chef Boy-Ar-Dee Homestyle) 85
  w/mushrooms, in jars (Heinz) 92
  w/mushrooms, mix, prepared* (Durkee) 61
  w/tomato and ground beef, mix, prepared* (Chef Boy-Ar-Dee) 109
Stroganoff sauce, canned (Contadina) 68
sweet and sour sauce, bottled (Kraft Sweet 'n Sour) 259
sweet and sour sauce, canned (Contadina) 148
sweet and sour sauce, canned (La Choy) 244
sweet and sour sauce, mix, prepared* (Durkee) 77
Swiss steak sauce, brown, canned (Compliment) 30
Swiss steak sauce, tomato, canned (Compliment) 34
tomato sauce, canned (Stokely-Van Camp) 35
tomato sauce, w/bits, canned (Hunt's) 41

sauces and gravies, continued

tomato sauce, w/onions, canned (Hunt's)	51
turkey gravy, mix, prepared* (French's)	46
turkey gravy, mix, prepared* (McCormick)	41
white sauce, mix, prepared* (Kraft)	197

** According to package directions*

CONDIMENTS & SEASONINGS, 1 tablespoon, except as noted

See also Chapter 12

	CALORIES
bacon bits, imitation:	
(Bac*os)	29
(Durkee)	24
(McCormick)	21
w/onion flakes (Lawry's Baconion)	35
chili powder (Mexene)	24
chutney, Major Grey's (Cresca)	49
chutney sauce (Spice Island)	36
herbs, blended (Lawry's Pinch of Herbs), ½ tsp.	4
horseradish dressing (Reese)	54
hot sauce (Frank's Red Hot), ¼ tsp.	tr.
meat sauce (Cresca O.K. Steak Sauce)	16
meat sauce (Cresca O.K. Spicy Steak Sauce)	11
meat sauce (Spice Island)	24
mint jelly (Crosse & Blackwell)	51
mint jelly, w/leaves (Reese)	58
mustard:	
brown (French's Brown 'N Spicy)	17
hot (Cresca English)	25
hot (Mister Mustard)	9
yellow (Kraft—all varieties)	12
w/horseradish (Best Foods)	9
w/horseradish (French's)	17
mustard sauce (Spice Island)	39
pepper, lemon (Durkee), ½ tsp.	3
pepper, lemon, marinade (Lawry's), ½ tsp.	4
salad seasoning (Durkee)	12
salad seasoning, w/cheese (Durkee)	30
salt, imitation butter flavor (Durkee), 1 tsp.	3

sandwich spread (Bama) 51
seafood cocktail sauce:
(Bernstein's of Long Beach) 35
(Crosse & Blackwell) 21
(Reese) 16
(Sau-Sea) 16
seasoning, mix (G. Washington Brown), 1 packet 6
seasoning, mix (G. Washington Golden), 1 packet 5
shrimp cocktail sauce (Crosse & Blackwell) 18
soy sauce (Chun King All Purpose) 6
soy sauce, Japanese-style (Chun King) 6
sweet and sour sauce (Chun King) 51
taco sauce (Old El Paso) 3
tartar sauce (Best Foods) 75
tartar sauce (Reese) 72
tartar sauce (Seven Seas) 78
teriyaki sauce (Chun King) 12
Worcestershire sauce (French's) 6

READY-TO-SERVE PUDDINGS, ½ cup, except as noted

See also Chapter 13

CALORIES

butterscotch:
canned (Betty Crocker) 171
canned (Hunt's Snack Pack) 238
dairy-packed (Sealtest) 124
frozen (Cool 'n Creamy) 204
in jars (Mott's Snack Pack) 225
caramel, canned (Rich & Ready) 184
cherry-vanilla, canned (Mott's Snack Pack) 225
chocolate:
canned (Betty Crocker) 175
canned (Hunt's Snack Pack) 234
canned (Rich & Ready) 191
dairy-packed (Sealtest) 136
frozen (Cool 'n Creamy Dark) 203
frozen (Cool 'n Creamy Light) 201
in jars (Mott's Snack Pack) 225
chocolate fudge:
canned (Betty Crocker) 175

chocolate fudge pudding, continued
canned (Hunt's Snack Pack) 229
canned (Rich & Ready) 186
in jars (Mott's Snack Pack) 225
custard, egg, dairy-packed (Sealtest) 149
lemon, canned (Betty Crocker) 198
lemon, canned (Hunt's Snack Pack) 175
lemon, in jars (Mott's Snack Pack) 225
plum pudding (Richardson & Robbins), 4 oz. 304
rice, canned (Betty Crocker) 154
rice, in jars (Lord Mott's) 148
tapioca, dairy-packed (Sealtest) 130
vanilla:
canned (Betty Crocker) 170
canned (Hunt's Snack Pack) 238
canned (Rich & Ready) 192
dairy-packed (Sealtest) 125
frozen (Cool 'n Creamy) 197
in jars (Mott's Snack Pack) 225

FROZEN DESSERT PIES, 1 whole pie*

See also Chapter 14

CALORIES

fruit and custard varieties, 8" diameter:
apple (Morton), 22 oz. 1548
apple (Morton), 24 oz. 1620
apple (Mrs. Smith's), 26 oz. 1820
apple crumb, Dutch (Mrs. Smith's), 26 oz. 1955
apple, tart, Dutch (Mrs. Smith's), 26 oz. 1595
blackberry (Banquet), 20 oz. 1504
blackberry (Mrs. Smith's), 26 oz. 1730
blueberry (Morton), 20 oz. 1440
blueberry (Mrs. Smith's), 26 oz. 1730
boysenberry (Morton), 22 oz. 1638
cherry (Morton), 22 oz. 1680
cherry (Morton), 24 oz. 2052
cherry (Mrs. Smith's), 26 oz. 1645
custard, coconut (Morton), 20 oz. 1230
custard, coconut (Morton), 22 oz. 1356
custard, coconut (Mrs. Smith's), 25 oz. 1635

custard, egg (Mrs. Smith's), 25 oz. 1485
lemon (Mrs. Smith's), 26 oz. 2125
lemon meringue (Mrs. Smith's), 20 oz. 1725
mince (Morton), 20 oz. 1476
mince (Mrs. Smith's), 26 oz. 2010
peach (Morton), 20 oz. 1414
peach (Morton), 22 oz. 1632
peach (Morton), 24 oz. 1710
peach (Mrs. Smith's), 26 oz. 1795
pecan (Morton), 20 oz. 2058
pecan (Mrs. Smith's), 24 oz. 2530
pineapple (Mrs. Smith's), 26 oz. 1830
pineapple cheese (Mrs. Smith's), 26 oz. 1640
pumpkin (Morton), 20 oz. 1000
pumpkin custard (Mrs. Smith's), 26 oz. 1375
raisin (Mrs. Smith's), 26 oz. 1890
strawberry (Morton), 20 oz. 1518
strawberry-rhubarb (Mrs. Smith's), 26 oz. 1875

fruit and custard varieties, 9" diameter:

apple (Mrs. Smith's Old Fashioned), 38 oz. 3050
blackberry (Mrs. Smith's Old Fashioned), 38 oz. 2850
blueberry (Mrs. Smith's Old Fashioned), 38 oz. 2850
cherry (Mrs. Smith's Old Fashioned), 38 oz. 2870
peach (Mrs. Smith's Old Fashioned), 38 oz. 3035
strawberry-rhubarb (Mrs. Smith's Old Fashioned), 38 oz. 2690

fruit and custard varieties, 10" diameter:

apple (Banquet), 46 oz. 3229
apple (Morton Home Style), 46 oz. 3088
apple (Mrs. Smith's Golden Deluxe), 46 oz. 3200
apple crumb (Mrs. Smith's Golden Deluxe), 46 oz. 3430
blackberry (Banquet), 46 oz. 3459
blackberry (Mrs. Smith's Golden Deluxe), 46 oz. 3035
blueberry (Banquet), 46 oz. 3367
blueberry (Morton Home Style), 46 oz. 3456
blueberry (Mrs. Smith's Golden Deluxe), 46 oz. 3035
cherry (Banquet), 46 oz. 3238
cherry (Morton Home Style), 46 oz. 3312
cherry (Mrs. Smith's Golden Deluxe), 46 oz. 2890
custard (Banquet), 46 oz. 2521
custard, coconut (Banquet), 46 oz. 2705
custard, coconut (Morton Home Style), 46 oz. 3960
custard, coconut (Mrs. Smith's Golden Deluxe), 44 oz. 2750

fruit and custard pies, 10" diameter, continued

lemon meringue (Mrs. Smith's Golden Deluxe), 36 oz.	3025
mince (Banquet), 46 oz.	3689
mince (Morton Home Style), 46 oz.	4179
mince (Mrs. Smith's Golden Deluxe), 46 oz.	3650
peach (Banquet), 46 oz.	2944
peach (Morton Home Style), 46 oz.	3192
peach (Mrs. Smith's Golden Deluxe), 46 oz.	3150
pecan (Mrs. Smith's Golden Deluxe), 36 oz.	3720
pumpkin (Banquet), 46 oz.	2815
pumpkin (Morton Home Style), 46 oz.	3904
pumpkin custard (Mrs. Smith's Golden Deluxe), 44 oz.	2370
pineapple cheese (Mrs. Smith's Golden Deluxe), 46 oz.	2730
strawberry-rhubarb (Mrs. Smith's Golden Deluxe), 46 oz.	3290
cream varieties, 8" diameter:	
banana (Morton), 14 oz.	1033
banana (Mrs. Smith's), 13 oz.	1160
blueberry (Morton Fruit 'n Creme Delight), 18¼ oz.	979
cherry (Morton Fruit 'n Creme Delight), 18¼ oz.	992
chocolate (Mrs. Smith's), 13 oz.	1285
chocolate nut (Kraft Chocolate Velvet Nut), 16¾ oz.	1809
coconut (Morton), 14 oz.	1112
coconut (Mrs. Smith's), 13 oz.	1225
lemon (Morton), 14 oz.	1056
lemon (Mrs. Smith's), 13 oz.	1165
mint (Kraft Mint Mist), 13 oz.	1300
Neapolitan (Morton), 14 oz.	1032
Neapolitan (Mrs. Smith's), 13 oz.	1255
peppermint (Kraft Pink Peppermint), 13 oz.	1313
pineapple (Morton Fruit 'n Creme Delight), 18¼ oz.	1280
strawberry (Morton Fruit 'n Creme Delight), 18¼ oz.	1025
strawberry (Mrs. Smith's), 13 oz.	1180

* *Note variations in size and weight*

READY-TO-USE PIE FILLINGS & PIE SHELLS

See also Chapters 13 and 14

	CALORIES
pie fillings, fruit, 1 whole can or jar*:	
apple (Comstock), 21 oz.	695
apple (Mott's), 25 oz.	851
apple (Musselman's), 24 oz.	678
apple (Stokely-Van Camp), 22 oz.	600
apple (Wilderness), 21 oz.	627
apple, French (Comstock), 21 oz.	639
apricot (Comstock), 21 oz.	613
blackberry (Comstock), 21 oz.	855
blueberry (Comstock), 21 oz.	649
blueberry (Mott's), 25 oz.	800
blueberry (Musselman's), 24 oz.	678
blueberry (Stokely-Van Camp), 22 oz.	778
blueberry (Wilderness), 21 oz.	722
boysenberry (Comstock), 21 oz.	725
cherry (Comstock), 21 oz.	652
cherry (Mott's), 25 oz.	964
cherry (Musselman's), 24 oz.	678
cherry (Stokely-Van Camp), 22 oz.	770
cherry (Wilderness), 21 oz.	722
lemon (Comstock), 22 oz.	714
mincemeat (Comstock), 22 oz.	886
mincemeat (Borden's None Such), 18 oz.	972
mincemeat (Crosse & Blackwell), 18 oz.	1646
mincemeat, w/rum and brandy (Borden's None Such), 18 oz.	1058
peach (Comstock), 21 oz.	715
peach (Musselman's), 24 oz.	678
peach (Stokely-Van Camp), 22 oz.	1114
pineapple (Comstock), 21 oz.	547
pineapple (Wilderness), 21 oz.	606
pumpkin (Comstock), 29.4 oz.	873
pumpkin (Stokely-Van Camp), 18 oz.	726
raisin (Comstock), 22 oz.	744
raspberry, red (Comstock), 21 oz.	832
strawberry (Comstock), 21 oz.	621

ready-to-use pie fillings and pie shells, continued

pie shells, frozen, 1 package*:

plain, 8"-diameter (Morton)	737
plain, 9" diameter (Mrs. Smith's)	1100
plain, 10" diameter (Mrs. Smith's)	1240
honey graham, 10" diameter (Mrs. Smith's)	920

* *Note variations in size*

DESSERT & COFFEE CAKES, 1 whole cake*

See also Chapter 14

	CALORIES
almond (Sara Lee Coffee Ring), 10 oz.	1106
angel food (Howard Johnson's), 9 oz.	709
apple Danish (Morton), 13½ oz.	1129
apple Danish (Sara Lee Coffee Cake), 14 oz.	1176
apricot Danish (Sara Lee Coffee Cake), 14 oz.	1176
banana, frosted (Sara Lee), 14 oz.	1442
blueberry (Sara Lee Coffee Ring), 10 oz.	1080
butter streusel (Sara Lee Coffee Cake), 12½ oz.	1393
cherry Danish (Sara Lee Coffee Cake), 14 oz.	1050
chocolate, frosted (Sara Lee), 13½ oz.	1377
chocolate, German, frosted (Morton), 13 oz.	1360
chocolate, German, frosted (Sara Lee), 13½ oz.	1229
cinnamon-nut Danish (Sara Lee Coffee Cake), 11 oz.	1313
cinnamon-raisin Danish (Horton), 14 oz.	1461
cinnamon-sugar (Morton Melt-A-Way Coffee Cake), 13 oz.	1511
coconut, frosted (Pepperidge Farm), 17 oz.	1938
crumb (Drake's Coffee Cake), 11 oz.	1463
devil's food, frosted (Sara Lee), 14 oz.	1496
golden, frosted (Pepperidge Farm), 17 oz.	1920
golden, frosted (Sara Lee), 14 oz.	1442
lemon (Drake's Coffee Ring), 13 oz.	1028
maple crunch (Sara Lee Coffee Ring), 10 oz.	1157
orange, frosted (Sara Lee), 14 oz.	1442
pecan (Drake's Coffee Ring), 13 oz.	1109
pecan Danish (Morton Twist), 12 oz.	1369
pecan Danish (Sara Lee Coffee Cake), 6½ oz.	759
pound, plain (Drake's), 9 oz.	892
pound, plain (Howard Johnson's), 16 oz.	1723

pound, plain (Morton), 12 oz. 1407
pound, plain (Sara Lee), 12 oz. 1320
raspberry (Drake's Coffee Ring), 13 oz. 1028
raspberry (Sara Lee Coffee Ring), 10 oz. 1090

** Note variations in size*

CAKE MIXES & READY-TO-SPREAD FROSTINGS

See also Chapter 14

CALORIES

cakes, prepared*, 1 whole cake:
- applesauce-raisin (Duncan Hines) 1800
- banana (Betty Crocker Chiquita) 2464
- banana (Swans Down) 2152
- caramel (Duncan Hines) 2424
- cherry (Duncan Hines) 2316
- cherry chip (Betty Crocker) 2381
- chocolate, deep (Duncan Hines) 2412
- chocolate, German (Betty Crocker) 2404
- chocolate, milk (Betty Crocker) 2382
- chocolate, sour cream (Betty Crocker) 2334
- chocolate, Swiss (Duncan Hines) 2412
- chocolate chip (Swans Down) 2448
- coconut (Duncan Hines) 2400
- devil's food (Betty Crocker) 2388
- lemon (Betty Crocker SunKist) 2420
- lemon (Duncan Hines) 2368
- lemon flake (Swans Down) 2268
- marble, fudge (Duncan Hines) 2313
- orange (Betty Crocker SunKist) 2417
- orange (Duncan Hines) 2369
- pineapple (Duncan Hines) 2369
- spice (Duncan Hines) 2317
- white (Betty Crocker) 2280
- yellow (Betty Crocker) 2422
- yellow, golden butter (Duncan Hines) 3287

frostings, 1 whole can (16½ ounces):
- butterscotch (Betty Crocker) 1971
- chocolate (Betty Crocker) 1938
- chocolate, milk (Betty Crocker) 1962

ready-to-spread cake frostings, continued

fudge, dark Dutch (Betty Crocker) 1841
lemon (Betty Crocker SunKist) 1986
vanilla (Betty Crocker) 1991

* *According to package directions, without frosting*

PASTRY & SWEET ROLLS, FROZEN OR REFRIGERATED

See also Chapter 14

	CALORIES
pastry, 1 piece, as packaged:	
apple dumpling (Pepperidge Farm)	276
apple tart (Pepperidge Farm)	276
apple turnover* (Pillsbury)	215
blueberry tart (Pepperidge Farm)	277
cherry tart (Pepperidge Farm)	277
cherry turnover* (Pillsbury)	188
chocolate tart (Pepperidge Farm)	310
coconut tart (Pepperidge Farm)	310
lemon tart (Pepperidge Farm)	317
lemon turnover (Pepperidge Farm)	341
peach dumpling (Pepperidge Farm)	293
peach turnover (Pepperidge Farm)	323
raspberry turnover (Pepperidge Farm)	337
strawberry turnover (Pepperidge Farm)	326
sweet rolls, 1 piece, as packaged:	
apple nut kuchen (Durkee Petite Danish)	59
caramel nut Danish (Durkee Petite)	103
caramel nut Danish* (Pillsbury)	165
cinnamon Danish* (Pillsbury)	156
cinnamon whirls (Durkee Petite Danish)	78
cinnamon rolls, iced* (Pillsbury)	130
honey buns (Morton)	170
lemon puffs (Durkee Petite Danish)	90
orange Danish, iced* (Pillsbury)	156

* *Prepared according to package directions*

SPECIALTY SNACK CAKES & PIES*

See also Chapter 14 and "Pastry & Sweet Rolls"

	CALORIES
brownies, pecan (Hostess), 2-oz. brownie	224
cake, chocolate, creme filled:	
(Drake's Chocolate Creme Cups), 1⅜-oz. cake	191
(Drake's Devil Dogs), 1¼-oz. piece	164
(Drake's Devil Dogs), 2¼-oz. piece	307
chocolate coated (Drake's Frosti Devils), 1¼-oz. cake	164
chocolate coated (Drake's Funny Bones), 1¼-oz. cake	164
chocolate coated (Drake's Ring Ding), 2½-oz. cake	366
chocolate coated (Drake's Ring Ding Jr.), 1⅓-oz. cake	186
vanilla coated (Drake's Yodels), ⅞-oz. roll	134
cake, coffee, crumb topped (Drake's Small), 2¼-oz. cake	321
cake, coffee, crumb topped (Drake's Jr.), 1.1-oz. cake	133
cake, pound, plain (Drake's), 1½-oz. slice	181
cake, pound, plain (Drake's All Butter Jr.), 1.1-oz. slice	104
cake, pound, plain (Drake's All Butter Jr.), 1½-oz. slice	142
cake, pound, raisin (Drake's), 1½-oz. slice	232
cake, yellow, creme filled:	
(Drake's Golden Creme Cups), 1⅜-oz. cake	172
chocolate coated (Drake's Golden Ring Ding), 2½-oz. cake	335
pie:	
apple (Drake's Fruit Doodle), 1⅝-oz. pie	178
apple (Hostess Apple Fried), 4-oz. pie	363
cherry (Drake's Fruit Doodle), 1⅝-oz. pie	173
cherry (Hostess Cherry Fried), 4-oz. pie	349
lemon (Hostess Lemon Fried), 4-oz. pie	368

* *Note variations in size*

COOKIES, 1 piece, as packaged

See also Chapter 14

	CALORIES
almond flavored (Stella D'Oro Breakfast Treats)	99
apple flavored (Sunshine Apple Coolers)	29
butter flavored (Jacob's Petit Beurre)	110
butterscotch-nut, refrigerator, baked (Pillsbury)	66

cherry flavored (Sunshine Cherry Coolers) 29
chocolate (Stella D'Oro Margherite) 73
chocolate chip (Keebler Old Fashioned) 79
chocolate chip (Keebler Rich 'n' Chips) 73
chocolate chip, refrigerator, baked (Pillsbury) 53
chocolate-coconut-pecan, iced (Keebler German Chocolate) 85
chocolate covered sandwich (Keebler Penguin) 113
chocolate-nut (Pepperidge Farm Old Fashioned Brownie) 54
chocolate-nut sandwich, vanilla filled (Pepperidge Farm Capri) 82
chocolate-nut sandwich, chocolate filled (Pepperidge Farm Rochelle) ... 81
coconut (Drake's Coconut Jumble) 78
coconut (Nabisco Bars) 45
coconut caramel, iced (Yum Yums) 83
creme sandwiches:
- assorted (Pride) 55
- chocolate (Keebler Keebies) 51
- chocolate fudge (Cookie Break) 53
- (Keebler Grammys) 50
- mint flavored (Mint Hydrox) 46
- (Social Tea Sandwich) 51
- vanilla (Cookie Break) 52

devil's food cake (Keebler Devilsfood) 64
egg kichel, sugared (Stella D'Oro Anginetti) 28
graham cracker, cinnamon (Keebler Cinnamon Crisp) 17
graham cracker, cinnamon (Sunshine Cinnamon Toast) 17
graham cracker, peanut butter covered (Keebler) 46
lemon flavored (Nabisco Jumble Rings) 70
lemon flavored (Pepperidge Farm Pirouettes) 37
lemon flavored (Sunshine Lemon Coolers) 29
mint flavored, chocolate covered (Nabisco Mint Sandwich) 88
oatmeal (Pepperidge Farm Old Fashioned Irish) 50
oatmeal, w/raisins, iced (Nabisco) 57
oatmeal, w/raisins, refrigerator, baked (Pillsbury) 55
oatmeal, whole-wheat (Drake's) 83
oatmeal-peanut sandwich (Sunshine) 90
peanut bars, cocoa covered (Crowns) 94
peanut butter (Keebler Old Fashioned) 81
peanut butter, refrigerator, baked (Pillsbury) 55
peanut butter sandwich, chocolate filled (Pepperidge Farm Nassau) 83
peanut creme, cocoa covered (Nabisco Fancy Patties) 198
peanut creme, cocoa covered (Nabisco Peanut Creme Sticks) 48
pecan sandwich, creme filled (Pepperidge Farm Dresden) 83

shortbread (Keebler Stars) 35
shortbread (Pepperidge Farm Old Fashioned) 72
shortbread, almond (Keebler Spiced Windmill) 61
spice (Nabisco Wafers) 33
(Stella D'Oro Angelica Goodies) 100
(Stella D'Oro Como Delight) 153
sugar (Pepperidge Farm Old Fashioned) 51
sugar, brown (Pepperidge Farm Old Fashioned) 48
sugar, refrigerator, baked (Pillsbury) 61
sugar wafers, all flavors (Keebler Krisp Kreem) 31
vanilla:
  (Nilla Wafers) 18
  (Pepperidge Farm Pirouettes) 37
  (Stella D'Oro Margherite) 73
  chocolate-laced (Pepperidge Farm Pirouettes) 38
  sandwich, chocolate filled (Pepperidge Farm Lido) 91
  sandwich, chocolate filled (Pepperidge Farm Milano) 62
  sandwich, mint creme filled (Pepperidge Farm Mint Milano) 76
  chocolate coated (Pepperidge Farm Orleans) 30

JELLIES, PRESERVES & PEANUT BUTTER, 1 tablespoon

See also Chapters 15 and 18

CALORIES

apple butter (Bama) 31
apple butter (Ma Brown) 32
apple butter (Musselman's) 33
jam:
  all flavors, except apricot, peach, pear and plum (Bama) 54
  apricot, peach, pear and plum (Bama) 51
  grape (Welch's Grapelade) 55
  strawberry (Musselman's) 54
jelly, all flavors (Bama) 51
jelly, all flavors (Musselman's) 53
jelly, all flavors (Welch's) 50
marmalade, orange (Bama) 54
marmalade, orange (Ma Brown) 49
marmalade, orange (Welch's) 55
preserves:
  all flavors, except apricot, peach, pear and plum (Bama) 54
  all flavors, except peach (Welch's) 55

preserves, continued

apricot, peach, pear and plum (Bama)	51
peach (Welch's)	50
quince (Reese)	55
wild blueberry (Reese)	55
wild strawberry (Reese)	55
peanut butter:	
(Bama)	100
(Smucker's)	104
w/jelly (Bama)	82
w/jelly (Smucker's Goober)	85

CANDY, 1 ounce

See also Chapter 16

	CALORIES
(Black Cow Sucker)	103
butterscotch (Nestlé's Morsels)	150
caramel (Whirligigs)	112
caramel, chocolate (Sugar Daddy Jrs.)	113
cherries, dark chocolate covered (Nabisco)	115
cherries, milk chocolate covered (Nabisco)	108
chocolate, solid:	
milk (Hershey Chips)	152
milk (Kraft Stars)	147
milk (Lindt)	160
milk (Nestlé's Morsels)	143
milk (Nabisco Stars)	153
mint (Nabisco Mint Wafers)	169
semisweet (Ghirardelli Chips)	146
semisweet (Hershey Chips)	145
semisweet (Lindt—Squares)	140
semisweet (Lindt Excellence)	162
semisweet, w/vanilla (Lindt)	163
sweet (Hershey Sprigs)	136
chocolate, candy coated (M & M's)	130
chocolate, w/almonds (Gala Bar—milk chocolate)	149
chocolate, w/almonds (Gala Bar—sweet milk chocolate)	153
chocolate, w/hazelnuts (Gala Bar)	149
chocolate, w/malted milk bits (Nabisco Crunch)	150
coconut (Stuckey's Pralines)	125

coconut, chocolate covered (Hershey Coconut Cream Egg) 142
coconut, chocolate covered (Nabisco Squares) 120
fudge, chocolate or vanilla (Stuckey's) 121
fudge, chocolate, w/black walnuts (Stuckey's) 128
fudge, chocolate, chocolate covered, w/nuts (Nabisco) 132
fudge roll, w/caramel and peanuts (Oh Henry—2 lb. size) 145
hard candy:
  all flavors (Jolly Rancher Stix Bars) 102
  all flavors (Jolly Rancher Stix Kisses) 110
  all flavors (Jolly Rancher Stix Pak) 128
  butterscotch (Nabisco Skimmers) 113
  cherry, wild (Nabisco Drops) 110
  chocolate (Nabisco Drops) 118
jellied candy, all flavors, chocolate covered (Kraft Bridge Mix) 120
malted milk balls, chocolate covered (Kraft) 137
maple (Stuckey's Praline) 125
marshmallows, white (Kraft Jet Puff—miniature) 92
marshmallows, coconut, toasted (Kraft Jet Puff) 107
marshmallows, flavored (Kraft Jet Puff—miniature) 92
mints, afterdinner, assorted (Merri-Mints) 100
mints, chocolate covered:
  (Junior) 90
  (Nabisco Peppermint Patties) 122
  (Nabisco Thin) 122
  (Richardson Peppermint Patties) 106
(Nabisco Bridge Mix) 123
nut brittle, peanut (Stuckey's) 122
nut brittle, peanut-coconut (Kraft) 125
(Nutty Crunch) 133
nuts, chocolate covered, peanut (Nabisco) 159
nuts, chocolate covered, peanut, candy coated (M & M's) 130
nuts and caramel, chocolate covered, pecan roll (Stuckey's Log) 135
peanut butter, chocolate covered (Reese's Peanut Butter Eggs) 135
peanut butter crunch (Nabisco) 122
raisins, chocolate covered (Nabisco) 120
(Rally Bar) 125
(3 Musketeers) 120

ICE CREAM & FROZEN CONFECTIONS, ½ pint, except as noted

See also Chapter 16

	CALORIES
frozen dessert, all flavors, mix, prepared* (Junket Freezing Mix)	198
ice bars:	
all fruit flavors (Borden's Twin Pops), 3 fl. oz.	76
all fruit flavors (Eskimo Pie Twin Pops), 3 fl. oz.	62
all fruit flavors (Good Humor Whammy-Stix), 1¾ fl. oz.	40
all fruit flavors (Sealtest Twin Pops), 3 fl. oz.	70
chocolate (Popsicle), 3 fl. oz.	106
root beer (Popsicle), 3 fl. oz.	70
ice cream:	
all flavors, 10% fat (Borden's)	261
all flavors, 10% fat (Pet)	238
all flavors, 14% fat (Lady Borden)	337
chocolate, 9.15% fat (Foremost)	262
chocolate, 9.8% fat (Sealtest)	272
chocolate, 14.5% fat (Prestige French)	364
strawberry, 8.2% fat (Sealtest)	266
strawberry, 8.65% fat (Foremost)	242
vanilla, 10.2% fat (Sealtest Party Slice), 1 slice	133
vanilla, 10.35% fat (Foremost)	265
ice cream, non-dairy, chocolate, 10.71% fat (Dutch Pride)	266
ice cream, non-dairy, strawberry, 10.11% fat (Dutch Pride)	263
ice cream, non-dairy, vanilla, 10.65% fat (Dutch Pride)	270
ice cream bars, chocolate:	
chocolate coated (Good Humor), 3 fl. oz.	205
chocolate coated (Good Humor Whammy-Stix), 1¾ fl. oz.	140
chip, crunch coated (Good Humor Crunch), 3 fl. oz.	239
chip, crunch coated (Good Humor Whammy-Stix Crunch), 1¾ fl. oz.	202
ice cream bars, strawberry:	
chocolate coated (Good Humor Whammy-Stix), 1¾ fl. oz.	149
ripple, cake coated (Good Humor Strawberry Shortcake), 3 fl. oz.	235
ice cream bars, vanilla:	
chocolate coated (Borden's), 2½ fl. oz.	153
chocolate coated (Good Humor), 3 fl. oz.	202
chocolate coated (Good Humor Whammy-Stix), 1¾ fl. oz.	140
chocolate coated (Sealtest Miniature), 1½ fl. oz.	128
chocolate-toffee coated (Sealtest Toffee Crunch), 3 fl. oz.	149

sherbet coated (Sealtest Orange Creame), 2½ fl. oz. 103
toasted almond coated (Good Humor Toasted Almond), 3 fl. oz. 234
and fudge, cake coated (Good Humor Chocolate Eclair), 3 fl. oz. 217

ice cream cones, vanilla:
w/chocolate syrup and nuts (Eskimo Topper), 3 fl. oz. 182
w/chocolate syrup and nuts (Sealtest Choco-Nut Sundae), 2½ fl. oz. . .186

ice cream cup, vanilla (Good Humor), 3 fl. oz. 110
ice cream cup, vanilla w/chocolate syrup (Borden's), 3½ fl. oz. 142
ice cream sandwich, vanilla, w/wafers (Eskimo), 3 fl. oz. 186
ice cream sandwich, vanilla, w/wafers (Sealtest), 3 fl. oz. 173

ice milk:
all flavors, 3% fat (Pet) 170
all flavors, 4% fat (Pet) 208
buttered almond, 5.3% fat (Sealtest Light 'n Lively) 216
chocolate, 3.1% fat (Sealtest Light 'n Lively) 196
chocolate, 4.4% fat (Foremost Big Dip) 216
orange-pineapple, 2.9% fat (Sealtest Light 'n Lively) 188
peach, 2.6% fat (Sealtest Light 'n Lively) 188
strawberry, 3.7% fat (Foremost Big Dip) 211
vanilla, 3.1% fat (Sealtest Light 'n Lively) 190
vanilla, 4% fat (Borden's Lite Line) 216
vanilla, 4.2% fat (Foremost Big Dip) 219
vanilla-chocolate-strawberry, 3% fat (Sealtest Light 'n Lively) 192
vanilla fudge, 3.3% fat (Sealtest Light 'n Lively) 206

ice milk, non-dairy, chocolate, 7% fat (Dutch Pride) 210
ice milk, non-dairy, strawberry, 6.65% fat (Dutch Pride) 208
ice milk, non-dairy, vanilla, 7% fat (Dutch Pride) 213

ice milk bars:
chocolate, chocolate coated (Good Humor Whammy-Stix), 1¾ fl. oz. . .128
vanilla, chocolate coated (Borden's), 2½ fl. oz. 136
vanilla, chocolate coated (Good Humor Whammy-Stix), 1¾ fl. oz. 128
vanilla, sherbet coated (Dreamsicle), 2½ fl. oz. 69
vanilla, sherbet coated (Sealtest Orange Treat), 2½ fl. oz. 80

sherbet:
all fruit flavors, 1% fat (Borden's) 226
lemon, lime or orange, 1.2% fat (Foremost) 227
pineapple, 1.02% fat (Foremost) 221
raspberry, 1.05% fat (Foremost) 223

sherbet bar, chocolate fudge (Borden's), 2½ fl. oz. 80
sherbet bar, chocolate fudge (Good Humor Whammy-Stix), 1¾ fl. oz. . . .119
sherbet bar, chocolate fudge (Sealtest), 2½ fl. oz. 91

* *According to package directions*

FLAVORED MILK BEVERAGES, 8-ounce glass, except as noted

See also Chapter 4

	CALORIES
all flavors, mix, prepared* (Pet Instant Breakfast Plus)	290
cherry-vanilla, mix, prepared* (Foremost Instant Breakfast)	290
chocolate:	
drink, 0.7% fat, dairy-packed (Foremost)	161
drink, 2% fat, dairy-packed (Sealtest)	178
drink, canned (Stokely-Van Camp)	128
milk, 3.3% fat, dairy-packed (Foremost)	218
milk, 4% fat, dairy-packed (Borden's Dutch Chocolate)	280
milk, canned (Borden's Frosted Shake)	284
mix, prepared* (Knox Gelatin Drink), 6-oz. gls.	204
mix, prepared* (Pillsbury Instant Breakfast)	305
chocolate fudge, canned (Borden's Frosted Shake)	284
chocolate malted, mix, prepared* (Pillsbury Instant Breakfast)	305
coffee, canned (Borden's Frosted Shake)	286
egg nog, 6% fat, dairy-packed (Foremost)	412
egg nog, 6% fat, dairy-packed (Sealtest)	348
egg nog, 8% fat, dairy-packed (Sealtest)	384
egg nog, canned (Borden's Frosted Shake)	284
strawberry, canned (Borden's Frosted Shake)	283
strawberry, mix, prepared* (Pillsbury Instant Breakfast)	300
vanilla, canned (Borden's Frosted Shake)	282
vanilla, mix, prepared* (Pillsbury Instant Breakfast)	290

* *According to package directions*

SOFT DRINKS, 8-ounce glass

See also Chapters 3 and 19

	CALORIES
birch beer (Canada Dry)	104
blended flavors (Canada Dry Purple Passion)	113
blended flavors (Canada Dry Tahitian Treat)	133
blended flavors (Shasta Tiki)	113
cherry, black (Shasta)	117
cherry, wild (Canada Dry)	113

cola:
  (Canada Dry Jamaican) 102
  (Canada Dry Sport) 102
  (Cliquot Club) 109
  (Shasta) 103
  cherry flavored (Shasta) 103
cream soda (Canada Dry) 123
cream soda (Shasta) 113
ginger ale:
  (Canada Dry Golden) 85
  (Cliquot Club) 87
  (Santiba) 84
  (Shasta) 88
ginger beer (Canada Dry) 94
grape (Canada Dry Concord) 123
grape (Clicquot Club) 139
grape (Shasta) 117
grapefruit (Shasta Swing) 113
lemon-lime (Canada Dry) 120
lemon-lime (Shasta) 97
orange (Canada Dry Sunshine) 123
orange (Clicquot Club) 139
orange (Shasta) 128
orange-pineapple (Canada Dry Cactus Cooler) 113
quinine water (Santiba) 83
quinine water (Shasta) 76
raspberry, wild (Shasta) 117
root beer (Canada Dry Rooti) 103
root beer (Clicquot Club) 104
root beer (Shasta) 113
strawberry (Canada Dry) 113
strawberry (Shasta) 108

INDEX